A Summer Interrupted – 1939

The Remarkable Story of An Evacuee

G. Michael Burns

Propagator Press

This book is published by Propagator Press

Propagator Press
38 Parkside Road
Leeds
LS6 4NB

© G. Michael Burns 2011

The rights of G. Michael Burns to be identified as author of this work have been asserted by him in accordance with the Copyright, designs and Patents Act 1988.

All rights reserved. No part of this publication may be reproduced, stored in a retrieval system, or transmitted in any form or by any means, electronic, mechanical, photocopying, recording or otherwise without the prior written permission of the publishers.

ISBN   978-1-908037-15-2 Paperback
           978-1-908037-16-9 Hardback

Designed by Propagator Press
Printed in Great Britain

CONTENTS

Chapter		Page
	Foreword	1
	Introduction	3
	Author's Note	7
1	Peace in England	11
2	Platform to Hatch Beauchamp	21
3	The Manor House and a New Home	29
4	Getting On With It	33
5	Our First Christmas	39
6	Return to London – Hell from the Skies	43
7	After the Blitz – Return to the West Country	57
8	Everyday Life as an Evacuee	65
9	Important Visitors	85
10	Moments of Sadness	109
11	The Yanks – 1942	117
12	Romance Blossoms	125
13	VE – Day	137
14	American War Bride says Goodbye	153
15	Children and People of Hatch	169
16	70th Evacuee Reunion	175
17	A Son's Reflection	181
18	This England	185
	References	189

DEDICATION

- To my mother whose courage I learned from and whose life has been a message to us all. You will always have my admiration and love and without you, there would have been no Summer Interrupted to learn about.

- To my two Uncles, Dennis and Charles, and my Aunt Marie, three of the bravest people I have ever known......and to all evacuees everywhere for your sacrifices throughout the War.

- To the biggest fan and supporter in my life, my wife, Pam. I will spend every day saying thank you, without your help none of this would have been possible.

- To Keith, my brother.

- To Stan and Propagator Press for your encouragement and support in producing this book.

Foreword

All my life I have heard my mother, Eileen Burns' stories. Stories told over Sunday dinner, or when my parents reminisced about the war over a glass of wine. She would tell how she and her brothers and sister had to grow up quickly as a result of the war and of being torn away from her parents during the Evacuation and arriving in Hatch Beauchamp, near Taunton in Somerset, where she spent six years in an idyllic English Manor House called Hatch Court. This was supposedly a "quiet and safe" part of The West Country, but, as a school girl walking to and from school, she still had to keep an eye open for the German fighters and bombers which sometimes strayed into her "safe" life. Indeed, no matter where they lived, no-one in Britain could be said to be truly safe at that time.

Later, she worked as a parlour-maid, serving dinner to the famous and near famous of the British and Canadian military and even Churchill's Cabinet Ministers!

Eileen's life as a young girl was anything but ordinary. Not many evacuees spoke to an important American General on the phone, or sent a Canadian General to the servants' entrance of the house, thinking he was a tradesman. Much less told the Minister of Information and the Minister of Aircraft Production, both members of Winston Churchill's war cabinet, to "Wait at the front door while I find the lady of the house" (not knowing who they were). Very few young girls have danced with an RAF Air Chief Marshal, while standing on his boots.

Then there was the arrival of the exciting Americans; the American soldiers who had come to England to "See where the hell this god-damned war is." She told me how she met, fell in love, and ultimately married my father, one of those exciting Americans and how, at 19 years of age, she boarded a ship and sailed to America, to begin life as one of the 83,000 English war brides.

For 56 years, I have had the unique opportunity to talk to this lady, who my friends have always called a "piece of living history," about her life. This story is based on a son's love for his mother and admiration for a life that has been fascinating, unique and filled with heartbreak and touching stories and experiences that only happen once in a lifetime. My late father put my mother's life during the war into perspective years ago. He said, "Your mother's life in those six years was more exciting than mine in 50 years."

She is 84 now, her memory is fading somewhat and, before the events become only a story I had heard at dinner, they need to be told and remembered, if for no other reason than all generations should remember and realize that the people who made that history still walk amongst us.

They may be slightly slower, a little hard of hearing, hair no longer grey but white, but remarkable people, nevertheless.

Many stories of evacuees from wartime London and other major British cities, have been told by respected authors and those who lived during that time .The lives of the civilians and soldiers, the members of that fraternity of 'the greatest generation', have been chronicled in numerous worldwide bestsellers. Many of those books have magnificently and movingly held readers such as me, spellbound about life during the war. But maybe one more book can remind us that there are still many stories yet to be told about these remarkable people. All you have to do is make the journey back; back to a "Summer Interrupted – 1939."

Introduction

Going Home

Many times over the past ten years, I have told my mother that if she ever wanted to return to her home, in England, we would go. Her answer was always, *"No."* Being the oldest of four children and having lost her beloved sister, Marie, and her twin brothers, Dennis and Charles, there was no reason for her to return. She said, *"All that I have loved about England is in the past or gone forever."*

Then, in October of 2008, we heard about the 70th Reunion of Evacuees that was to be held in September 2009 at St. Paul's Cathedral in London. I said to my mother, "Mom, if you would like to go back, I will take you." To my surprise she quietly said, *"I would like to go back one more time and see my home."*

And so we did. In August 2009, I sat impatiently in the Admiral's Club in the Dallas Fort Worth airport with my wife, Pam, and my mother, Eileen, waiting to board Flight 50 from Dallas to Heathrow Airport in London. As I sat looking across the table at my mother while she read the newspaper, I wondered what this return to England would mean to her. She was 83 years old, hard of hearing, and her memory was not what it used to be. She is, however, even at this age, as sharp as they come.

I have been told by many senior citizens over the years, that with age comes an understanding of how a life has been lived and your experiences in that life become what you want them to be, good or bad. I think you try to let the not- so- pleasant memories drift from your mind and the times you try to focus on are those that have changed your life, brought you joy, or are etched in your memory as events that one never forgets.

As I drank my cup of coffee and looked at this elderly lady, I wondered if this was how she might be thinking. We were taking her back to England one more time, so she could join in the Evacuees Remembrance Day Celebration at St Paul's Cathedral in London on the 70th anniversary of the start of WWII. She would be one of many adults who were evacuated from their homes in what the British government had named "Operation Pied Piper."

As we waited for our flight to be called, I asked my mother if she was excited about going home again. She said, *"Although your father and I have returned to England many times over the past 25 years, this trip means more to me than any other."* She knew this would be her last trip and she would be a part of something that most of us have forgotten, never heard of and, in this age of revisionist history, is fading from books, and people's memories.

I knew how truly special this trip would be for all of us. Not many 56 year old men and their wives take vacations with their mothers, but, this was one trip I desperately wanted to be a part of. I would be able to witness a page of history that I had heard and read about most of my adult life, my mother's war. And to be able to witness what it must have seemed like for her that day in August 1939, when, aged 12, she stood on the platform at the train station with her twin brothers, Dennis and Charles and her sister, Marie, and waved goodbye to her parents.

For my wife, Pam, and me, it would also be a trip of a lifetime. My mother is like many women of her generation; her own life had always taken second place to her husband and children. As we were growing up, she sacrificed much for my brother, Keith, and me and, frankly, sacrificed too much for my father. But this time it would be different, she would be the centre of attention. Our family in the United States and in England had seen to that.

The coming 16 days would be about her. For the first time in her life we were determined to make sure that this journey to England would be her trip and we were going to see to it that whatever she wanted to do, we did. In a small way, we were trying to give her back a piece of her childhood that she had lost because of the war.

When I asked her if she was excited about going back to England, she said, *"Yes,"* with a touch of sadness in her voice, so I asked her if something was wrong. She answered, *"No, I just wish Dennis, Charles and Marie were still alive, because they would have enjoyed the day at Saint Paul's so much. They really had a hard time dealing with the evacuation."* It was so typical of my mother that she was thinking of her brothers and sister, not of herself. She was the oldest of the family and to have lost all her younger siblings over the past few years still weighed heavily on her mind. I looked at my wife, shook my head, got up from my seat and went to check the departure board; (it doesn't look good for grown men to have tears in their eyes in airport lounges).

Once we were airborne and on our way to London, I went to where my mother was seated, enjoying a glass of wine and sat down next to her to ask her how she was enjoying the flight. I noticed she was busily filling out a luggage tag, the kind that people used to put on their luggage back in the 30s and 40s. When I asked what she was doing, she looked at me and said, *"I'm filling out an evacuee tag that the Evacuee Association sent me for the service at St. Paul's."* I asked to see it and on the tag, she had written her name, the school she attended in 1939, her home address in 1939 and the train station she left from when she was evacuated over 70 years ago.

As I read the information she said proudly, *"I'm going to wear that when we get to St Paul's in London. I think others who attend will do the same."* I laughed and said, "Sure mom, that's great," but thought to myself how silly she would look, standing in front of the world famous Cathedral with this tag hanging from her coat. (How surprised I would be!). I got up to return to my seat.

As I turned around, my mother was proudly looking at the information she had written on the cardboard tag. I noticed a look on her face I had not often seen. It was the look of someone lost in faraway thoughts and smiling to herself. I would see that look and smile many times in the coming three weeks. I sat in my seat and thought how excited and proud she seemed. This would be a trip everyone would remember.

As we flew through the night, I found myself wondering again what it must have been like to grow up in such a frightening, but exciting, time as the early 1940s. My mother had always told me that, bad as it was, it was also the most exciting time of her life and that applied for millions of others who grew up during the war. I have learned that the history of wars is almost always told by those who were on the winning side and that, in most cases, battles have been glamourized. Generals are turned into larger than life warriors and the enemy is almost always portrayed as brutal, heartless, evil men. WWII was no different. What did make this war different was the civilian population. Soldiers have always, and will always, do the fighting; they did in WWII, as they do today in far off mountains and deserts, but in the Second World War, it was not only the military who were the casualties, the civilians also suffered unspeakable tragedy and sorrow. I kept thinking what they must have experienced, often at a very young age, in France, Poland, Russsia and The Netherlands, or indeed, the cities across Great Britain.

More than anything else, however, I wondered, what my mother saw and lived through, and how the war changed her life forever.

I put down the book I was reading, got up from my seat and went back to check that my mother had settled down for the night. Most of those on board had fallen asleep and the only noise was the faint humming of the jet engines and I saw that, she too, was just beginning to doze off. As her eyes fluttered shut, she had a look on her face I had never seen before. It was a mixture of happiness and sadness and I realized that before we had even landed in London, my mother was already home. Memories of her childhood had already begun to take over.

Brigadier Andrew Hamilton Gault, DSO, ED, CD.
Owner of Hatch Court and Founder of Princess Patricia's

Author's Note

Millions of children were taken from their parents during 1939 to get away from the German bombing of London and other large British cities, which the Government knew was sure to come. My mother and her brothers and sister were similar to many other children. They were from the working people of London, with little or no knowledge of life in the country. What made their lives different, was where they were billeted and the special man and his wife who took 11 evacuees from London into their home on the 1st day of September 1939. For the next six years, they would live in a world unlike anything they could have imagined.

Brigadier A. Hamilton Gault and his wife, Dorothy, took these 11 evacuees to live in their huge manor house (Hatch Court) in Hatch Beauchamp Somerset.

At least five books have been written on this man and his extraordinary life and as I read them, I realized that much of what happened in my mother's life, and how her future was shaped, was the result of living at the home of Andrew Hamilton Gault and his wife. It is because of who he was that my mother had many of her experiences during the war. Some were good and exciting and some not so pleasant, but even in later life, her opinion of Gault and that of my late Uncles and Aunt, never wavered; they always said he was kind, a gentleman, and bigger than life.

My father, commenting on his first encounter with the Brigadier, said that in uniform or out, you knew he was "somebody." My dad said he reflected a bearing and demeanour of someone who had seen life at its best and worst.

Andrew Hamilton Gault was born in 1882 in Montreal, Canada, the son of one of Canada's wealthiest families. He was a successful businessman, who was involved in the family's dry goods and other businesses and helped to grow his family's wealth and prominence in Canada. But the family business was not Hamilton Gault's true interest. It was a military life which attracted him, beginning in the Boer War of 1899 (where he fought with the 2nd Canadian Mounted Rifles) and continuing for two more world wars. Not to overdramatize his life, Gault was a man of destiny. His performance in three wars seemed to fulfil that destiny and he left behind a legacy that is still strong and, a century later, not forgotten in Canada or, indeed, Great Britain.

In today's world, the words "bravery" and "hero" are overused and improperly assigned to feats accomplished in sports. Gault was brave and he was a hero. His decorations were numerous and he was awarded medals in three wars, by five foreign governments. He was wounded 5 times, losing his leg, receiving a serious hand wound and countless shrapnel wounds on the battlefield. If his life had ended there, he would have remained a famous soldier...but, that does not scratch the surface of his life or accomplishments.

The reasons my mother and others who came to Hatch Court were in awe of this man have been well documented. A brief summary of his accomplishments gives a better understanding of why the children who were evacuated to his estate in Hatch Beauchamp at the beginning of World War II met people of note, crossed paths with more Generals than most of us would ever hope to meet in two lifetimes and were treated better than many of the millions of other evacuees who covered the British countryside in those dark years of 1939-1945.

A. Hamilton Gault was the founder and financier of the legendary Princess Patricia's Canadian Light Infantry(named after the Duke of Connaught's daughter, Lady Patricia Ramsey) He is the last man in modern history to raise, finance, and equip an independent fighting force. In World War I, after service in the Boer War, Gault set out to equip a regiment of experienced, tough men who would serve the Empire on the fields of Europe. After much discussion in the Canadian War Office, he was given permission to embark on his dream; he took $100,000 of his own money (in those days a very considerable sum) and by late August of 1914 had achieved his goal. The full list of the Princess Patricia's wartime accomplishments is extensive, but suffice it to say, their heroic actions in Freezenburg, Mons, Sanctuary Wood, and other fields of battle in other wars led them to fame and glory and at the end of hostilities in WWI, the Princess Patricia's were selected to become part of Canada's Permanent Defence Force.

Gault was well-connected throughout his life; he counted numerous Canadian and British high ranking officers as friends, knew Prime Ministers of Britain and, during the Second World War, members of Churchill's war Cabinet. He counted two Kings of Great Britain as acquaintances. Gault was a member of the British House of Commons for Taunton for eleven years from 1924-1935. The town of Taunton made him a Freeman of the City, a rare honour for a Canadian.

In the mid-1920s, he purchased the estate known as Hatch Court as a wedding present for his wife, Dorothy, and this was to be his home for much of the remainder of his life. He was an avid flyer making trips throughout Europe. As war clouds gathered, a visit to Germany in the late 1930s earned him a meeting with Germany's military leaders including Field Marshal Hermann Goring and Germany's Fuehrer, Adolf Hitler.

Gault's military honours included a DSO, CD, MD (5 times), and in the First war after his actions on the battlefield there was a discussion of awarding him the Victoria Cross (Britain's highest military award) for heroism in battle. Additionally, in the King's Birthday Honours List of 3 June, 1919, he was appointed an Officer of the Order of the British Empire.

For unknown reasons he resigned the appointment. Wounded 5 times, he refused evacuation from the field of battle until his men were properly cared for. He was recalled to active duty in WW II as head of the Canadian Army's Replacement Forces, promoted to Brigadier in 1942, an accident led to his forced retirement in that year. Until his death in 1958 he maintained a home in Montreal Canada situated on Mt. Saint Hillarie. When he died he donated the house and the Mountain to McGill University.

It has been told to me over the years that my Aunt Marie adored this man, my Uncles, Dennis and Charles were in awe of him. My mother said he was and has remained the most fascinating person she ever met. It was because of Gault and his wife Dorothy and their willingness to even drive to London during the Blitz to get my mother, and her brothers and sister from London along with seven other children and return them to Hatch Beauchamp and Hatch Court to safety, that they had such deep feelings for this man. The Gaults drove to London to bring the children back, not something done by most people who had evacuees living with them, but unknown to the Brigadier that day my mother and siblings had already left for Taunton by train.

He cared enough for my mother that when my father and mother began to fall in love in 1943, he called my father's Commanding Officer and my dad to his house and bluntly told my father his intentions had better be honourable, and if Eileen was hurt by the relationship, my father would need to answer to him. Both my father and his CO remembered leaving the Brigadier's study that night and agreed this was not a man to be trifled with, and he wasn't even my mother's father. To say he took a personal interest in her family was an understatement. Throughout the war, important people visited the house and had discussions long into the night in his private study, the details of which are not known. But, for my mother and the children who called Hatch Court home during the war it was a refuge and a safe place. They were looked after by a man who with his wealth, reputation and history of bravery on the field of battle was not obligated during the war years to "babysit" 11 children from the streets of London.

Hamilton Gault and his wife, Dorothy, remained in touch with my parents until his death in 1958 and her death in 1972 and My Aunt Marie even spent a number of years of her life with the Gaults after the war. His funeral in Montreal (at which there were no fewer than a dozen General Officers, a Canadian Defence Minister and a provincial Governor General) served as a tribute by his country, ordinary soldiers both young and old came from all over Canada to pay their respects. General George Pearkes VC, who was at the funeral, told my Aunt, "If 'Hammie' (as he was known by his friends) was here he would be with the soldiers, he loved them more than any award or recognition he ever received, he always called them his boys."

Although a Major at the start of World War I, he was promoted to Lt. Colonel, Colonel, Regimental Colonel, and in World War II to Brigadier. For the purpose of this book and for simplicity he will throughout be referred to as the "Brigadier."

The Author

Author at Hatch Court Museum
to Princess Patricia's – 1985

Pam and Mike Burns on staircase
at Hatch Court - 1985

Chapter 1

Peace in England

During the late 1930s, life seemed normal to most people. My mother, her family and neighbours on Libra Road, in the East End of London, went about their daily lives as did almost everyone in Great Britain. My grandfather worked his jobs at a London meat market and on the docks along the River Thames. Certainly to a young girl of 11, the idea of a war that would turn her life and that of millions of others, upside down was more of a fantasy than a possibility. My mother has said that while adults talked about the "troubles" that seemed to be brewing on the European continent, it had no effect on what she considered to be important. Important to her was going to school, singing with her friends on street corners, and acting out a world of fantasy in school and neighbourhood plays.

While children played in the streets and went to school, the people of London, including the working class, went about their daily lives, trouble like no one could possibly envisage was, indeed, brewing in Europe. But even as a growing number of Members of Parliament began to speak out about unnerving events in Germany, life just went on.

My mother recalls:
I always have to laugh to myself in disbelief when people my age talk about how they were aware at such young ages that war was coming and they talk about how they felt. I was eleven. No child I knew was aware of the world situation or the appeasement process that Neville Chamberlin was engaging in. Of course, there were many children much smarter than me, and much better educated I'm sure, but the average young children in London were busy simply being children. War and politics was not something that many families talked about nightly at the dinner table. Our dinner discussions were conducted by my father and centred on his work, neighbours my mum shopped with, the world of Libra Road and the East End in which we lived. When my father talked politics it was most likely at the corner pub "The Libra Arms" with his friends. It seems funny all these years later that many people who were small children at the time have such vivid recollections of the world situation back in 1938. Their memories are certainly better than mine or my English friends I know today.

But what was occurring in the world was affecting them as they played in the streets, for what was taking place would end their world of innocence and games and change the lives of everyone forever.

By 1938 the Prime Minister of Great Britain was engaged in a game of diplomacy he had no chance of winning, trying to buy peace for England at any price. Unfortunately, Prime Minister Neville Chamberlain was willing to bargain for the peace he so desperately wanted with the world's best, but most evil, player on the world stage – Adolf Hitler. Quite simply, Chamberlain was not up to the game Hitler was playing, which was world domination. As Chamberlain would find out, Hitler was a master at bluff and intimidation.

Neville Chamberlain was a lifelong politician from one of Great Britain's most renowned political families. His family's fame rivalled (and at the time many thought surpassed) his parliamentary nemesis, Winston Churchill. Chamberlain was involved in a deadly game. A game he would ultimately lose and his name and reputation would be tarnished for thereafter.

The word most often associated with Chamberlain and what the people of Britain would bitterly remember during the dark days soon to come, was 'appeasement'. In order to appease Hitler and achieve 'Peace in our Time', he appears to have been willing to sell-out the citizens of virtually any country Hitler demanded, during the summer and fall of 1938. Despite this, less than a year later, Britain was at war.

It is not this author's intention to pass judgment on Neville Chamberlain in a story of a young girl and her life as an evacuee. However, one must understand the appeasement process that Chamberlain set in motion in 1938. Those were the events that brought war less than twelve months later to the country he so desperately tried to save. To many survivors of the London Blitz, Neville Chamberlain was as much to blame for their ordeal as were the Nazis of Hitler's Germany. One definition of appeasement is giving the bully what he wants. The problem with bullies is, they are seldom satisfied. Soon Londoners, like my grandmother, and many of my mother's friends would pay for that misjudgement with their lives.

My life as a child, growing up in the East End of London before the war, was, in many ways, fairly simple.

My mum and dad and the four of us kids lived at 1 Libra Road, Plaistow, London. We were poor, but didn't even know it. My dad worked on the docks and at Smithfield Meat Market. He worked so hard year in and year out. He worked different shifts, sometimes nights for 6 days a week steady. His meagre earnings were 7 pounds a month. How the six of us lived I will never know. The four of us kids always had nice clothes and we always seemed to have good food on the table. Looking back I can never remember my mother ever buying herself a new dress. I can remember when the twins were born, my mother changing her days to nights. She would let the boys sleep all day long so that my dad could sleep all day. She quietly turned her life around so she would work all night. Then she would be up all night when my dad would be working. She would clean and wash all night while those little boys would be crawling around everywhere. She had a hard life really. Sadly she died at the young age of 40.

My mother always described in great detail her house in Plaistow on Libra Road and the people on the street where she lived. In 1985, I was able to go to Libra Road with my mother and see for myself what was left of her home, her street and her early life.

My mother's house was not far from Plaistow station and travelling there on the London Underground, we saw signs for Bethnal Green, Bow, Stepney and Barking….all the names my mother had mentioned over the years as being part of the old East End. Outside Plaistow station, she seemed vaguely familiar with the area and talked of how, before the war, her father used to meet his friends for a pint at the Old Libra Arms, which really was only a stone's throw from their house on the corner. Everyone knew their neighbours. All the men worked on the London Docks, Woolwich Arsenal, Smithfield meat market or the factories around Dagenham.

As we walked down the street we stopped in front of rows of terrace houses. This type of house was built in the 1920s and 30s and made up a large portion of the houses outside the City of London. The same type of house still covers the area today. With the exception of tall apartment buildings that have been built since the war and were obviously not built for the purpose of adding beauty to the surroundings, at first glance little seemed to have changed.

My mother suddenly stopped in mid-stride and stared at the house on the end of the street. It was 1, Libra Road. A sense of happiness came over me. After all the years that had passed, my mother and I were at the house she grew up in, where, until the September of 1939, she lived a simple life with her family, went to school and played with her friends. I was thrilled, I looked over at my mother and said "Well mom how does it feel to be home?" She stared ahead, turned to me and said, *"This is not my house."* The old row of houses she knew had been torn down and smaller, single-storey houses, with little or no garden, stood in their place.

The Anderson Shelters that had saved so many people during the Blitz had long since been ploughed over and disappeared, just a memory to those who were there. I was stunned, "Not your home? This is 1 Libra Road." But she knew something was different. Still, at least one thing remained in 1985, the Old Libra Arms. It operated until 2007 and now in that building that held so many stories of local people's lives stands a corner market, the type of market you will find on many corners in the East End.

As a man passed by I stopped him and said, "Are these the original from before the war?" He said "No, I don't think so. Most of the houses were destroyed during the war and torn down when the war was over." My mother nodded her head. She had already told me that the last time she saw her house, most of the front was gone from the bombing and scaffolding was in front of the house to hold it up. We found out later that day it had indeed been torn down.

As we walked in the late July afternoon I asked her if had she seen enough. She looked at me and simply said, "I have seen too much." The old buildings now intermingled with the newer ones and the physical presence of where she had lived was gone forever. Her life as a child, and where she grew up was gone and for her, and for countless thousands of children like her, only the memories remain.

I guess I was a street urchin, not really, but I was always playing whip and top, marbles, cigarette cards and skipping rope. I had roller skates and a lot of us kids would skate for hours. I would skate around to the other streets and challenge the other kids to do the snake or some other fancy trick. I'd ride the trains and jump off at Bow station, run over the bridge and ride back to Plaistow. While it may seem rather tame today, train hopping was, for us, the height of excitement. I really loved being a kid in London. I was always in for everything and very, very daring. Some of the things I did were terrible, like kicking a poor woman's fence and making her chase us all around the streets. She found out where I lived, came to my house and told my mother what I had been doing. My mother smacked my face right in front of her. She had picked me out because of my curly blonde hair, but she never went to the other kids' parents. Needless to say, we never did that again.

I spent many hours on my own. I went to school, came home and just played in the streets. Our street was a wonderful place to live. There were lots of kids, all the neighbours were wonderful. People were poor, but everyone took care of everyone. When one man was out of work, either through a layoff or accident, the whole neighbourhood would take up a collection for his family. People shared what little they had. We all looked out for one another.

As children, we always looked forward to Guy Fawkes Day, November 5th. A group of us kids from the neighbourhood would get one of our dad's old suits and stuff it, making an effigy of Guy Fawkes, and put him in a pram or wheelbarrow. We would then take it up to Plaistow station and wait for the trains to come in around 6.00 o'clock when all the men would stream home. We would say "Please remember the Guy, Mister" and they would throw us money and we would share it. Then on Guy Fawkes Night, we would light a big bonfire in the garden, burn the Guy and set off all kinds of fireworks.

Guy Fawkes, or Bonfire Night, was (and still is) a celebration unique to England. Bonfire Night originated in 1605 from an attempt, by a group of disgruntled Englishmen, to blow up the Houses of Parliament. They decided King James I was mistreating those in England who followed the Roman Catholic religion, so Guy Fawkes and friends decided to put an end to this injustice. Their plan was simple. They would blow up the Houses of Parliament when King James I was attending a ceremony for the opening of Parliament, overthrow the British Monarchy and restore religious order and rights to the Catholics. Well, needless to say Guy Fawkes failed in his attempt. Unfortunately for Guy, the plot was discovered before the explosives could be set off, Guy Fawkes was arrested, hung, drawn and quartered and his remains were put on Traitors' Gate. It seems in those days justice was delivered in a more direct manner!

Before the War began, New Year's Eve celebrations were always special before midnight. A few People would bring their pianos out and we would all sing and dance in the street and at midnight, the bells would ring and the guns would fire at Woolwich Arsenal. Everyone in the street would join hands and sing 'Auld Lange Syne'. But the war would eventually change everything.

My school in London was Burks Senior Girls' School on Balaam Street, about six blocks from where I lived. We had wonderful teachers from 9am to 4:00pm each school day. During those hours we learned more in a day than children today learn in a year. We had religion, maths, English, elocution, literature, history, geography, knitting, needlework, sports, singing, country dancing, poetry, arts and crafts. I really loved my school even though everything was very strict. All of these wonderful things were taught to girls 11 years of age. We did marvellous plays and learned the classics. One year a group of us was picked to go to the Crystal Palace in London to perform before the Lord Mayor and Lady Mayoress of London. We sang beautiful songs. I was picked to recite a poem, and then six of us were picked to perform a series of minuets and other dances. I was so proud of myself. As a young girl I had dreams of a life of singing and dancing. Obviously they remained dreams.

I still remember when Olive Baxter had a tap dancing school near us in London 1935-1936. Naturally, all of us girls from our neighbourhood went every week for lessons. It cost a sixpence a lesson. We wore red and white checked dresses and red tap shoes.

As young girls, we looked forward to any event that was cause for parties and celebrations. While the well-to-do might have found countless reasons for balls and tableaux, in our neighbourhood, it needed to be an event of some importance which would allow my father to be home. The street on Libra Road would turn into what would today be considered a street party. All our neighbours on the street would set up tables, bring food, and one of our neighbours even brought their piano into the street, as they did at New Year. The event I remember best that caused all of this happiness and fun, was the Jubilee celebration of King George V in 1935.

King George V reigned as monarch from June 1911 until January 1936. He was a well loved, if a distant Monarch. The people of Great Britain, with its vast Empire, celebrated his Silver Jubilee in 1935 with magnificent parties. From Grand palaces throughout Britain and Government Houses throughout the commonwealth, to the simple celebrations from his less well- to-do subjects on thousands of streets like Libra Road in the East End, everyone took part.

Even though I was just a child, and my brothers and sister had no real recollection of the King's Jubilee, I can remember it well, not only because we children got to sing, dance and play in the street late into the night, but because to our amazement and disbelief early one evening both King George and Queen Mary came through our neighbourhood in the most magnificent gold and red trimmed coach I have ever seen. It was drawn by six beautiful white horses, with six mounted Household Calvary riders around the coach. The Monarchs waved to us as they slowly rode by. I believed then, as did all we kids, the King was waving directly at me. It was a moment that I always remembered and which has stayed with me to this day.

We lived down the street from the Libra Arms Pub and every Saturday night there would be singing and dancing in the Saloon bar. All of us kids used to walk down and sit on the curb and eat big sour pickles and chips (French fries). The Salvation Army was always there to preach and sing hymns outside the Libra Arms. One Saturday, the leader of the band in the Saloon Bar asked if any one of us children would stand on an orange crate and sing for a halfcrown. I was the only one to raise my hand. I stood on that box and sang 'There is a joy, joy, joy down in my heart' and 'Running over'. I used all the hand motions and naturally won the money and much praise. I was proud of myself when I took the money into the house and gave it to my mother.

During the summers, the regulars from the Libra Arms pub used to rent a big bus and take a day trip to Southend at the sea-side. We would wait for them to come back. As the bus came down Stratford Road, we could hear them singing. They would pull in after a day of celebration at the seaside and all of us kids would wait for the 'Penny scramble'. They would throw all their change up in the air and we would all scramble for the money. Needless to say with knees and elbows bleeding, I would scramble for my share.

One Saturday in 1937, I heard there was a talent show at the cinema on Plaistow Road. I didn't tell my parents, but took my red and white checked dress and tap shoes and off I went. I sang and danced and won 10 shillings! When my father found out, I got into trouble for not asking permission to go.

Every Sunday, Rosie Bolton (a friend of mine) and I would go over to the Red Lion Pub which was about a ½ mile from our house on the Barking Road. They had tables and chairs in the garden with a little stage set up in the back. Rosie and I used to sing and tap dance on that stage and had much fun. Years later when I returned to the Red Lion with my husband, and brother Dennis and his wife Janet, Dennis was extremely surprised when I told him I used to come here and sing and dance way before the war began. He said "Eileen, you were always a street urchin at heart." I guess he was right.

Every so often, a group of men in drag would turn up at the corner of our street with their barrel organ, and someone would shout 'Here Come the Fairies'! We would all sit on the kerb and these men would put on a show the likes of which you have never seen. They were dressed in beautiful clothes, high heels and makeup so that they looked like beautiful women. They would sing and dance for about an hour, then pass the hat round for a collection. The neighbours would put a few shillings in the hat then off they would go to the next street. Perhaps this seems out of place in today's world, but back then it was part of our neighbourhood entertainment.

The year 1939 began with the talk of war becoming more real and frantic whispered conversations between my parents in the lounge or kitchen became more frequent. As children we remained oblivious to what was taking shape. I remember that Marie had asked my mother a few times about other children talking about 'going away'. Her questions were quickly brushed aside by my mother as she told all of us everything was going to be fine. You have to remember these were the days when children were seen and not heard. What we did not know at the time was my parents had already been informed of a potential evacuation of children if war came.

On the other hand, as the summer of '39 moved England closer to war, I remained silent about what I heard from the snippets of conversation from my parents and neighbours, wondering what it could mean for me. I tried (for reasons I still can't explain) my hardest to put the thought of something terrible changing my life out of my mind. I knew things were changing in the world around me on Libra Road. It wasn't until my father returned from the local pub and handed my mother a pamphlet about building something called a 'bomb shelter' (Anderson Shelter) in the back garden that I felt a fear grow inside me, that was not to leave for six long years.

When the time came to build the Anderson Shelter we received the material for ours free, from the government, because my father's pay was not 5 pounds per week. When he worked at the Meat Packing company, as so many men were unemployed, they used him just enough to give him an income, as they had to give work hours to as many men as possible because times were so difficult in the East End. He always worked so hard.

But, when it came time to build the Shelter, he approached it as if it was the building of the Tower of London. He and my mum read the pamphlet over and over. I am not sure nor did I ever know if my dad could read very well, but he poured over the instructions nonetheless. He dug the hole and shored up the inside with wooden panels. He then fixed the "roof" tightly to the sides, and on each end placed the covers just so. My mother then took some supplies into the shelter, including the ever present Tilley lamp and placed an old piece of carpet on the floor to give it a sense of home.

I look back and think of the night that simple hole in the ground, covered by a piece of thin metal, saved our lives and remember how my mother and father would check every evening during the Blitz to see if the thin metal roof was still attached to the sides. For us, as children, it was a place of fun to play in and hide from each other, until the bombing started. Then it was our only means of survival on some terrible nights.

I knew years later the goodness of my father and mother and how hard they worked for so little. The building of the shelter has remained with me because for the first time that I could remember, I could no longer sit on the floor at my father's feet while he smoked his pipe. He became a man who took on a sense of urgency while building that shelter, in order to do what little he could to protect his family.

One day as I came home from Burks School on Ballam Street, where the local children played on the swings and playground, my mum was in our small back garden talking over the fence to our neighbour, Mrs Miller, while hanging laundry on the clothes line. As I stood beside my mum, asking her if I could go down the street to play, she seemed deep in conversation with the neighbour. They were talking about having enough food, how they would store food, what they would do if the shops closed? Things I had never heard my mother ask before.

As I asked her, for what seemed like the 10th time, if I could go play with my friends, she looked at me with the look only a mother can give their child and said, "Eileen dear, yes you may go and play, but come the moment I call, do not be late and do not leave our street, and, whatever you do, do not go anywhere near the railway tracks." She had a look of pure fear on her face, her voice was almost pleading in its tone. As I stared at her she leaned down and held me for a moment in her arms, she held me much tighter than I could ever remember, and she said "Now, go and play, but remember what I said." I left the back garden and ran through the house. It was late August, a beautiful sunny, late summer's day.

I really do think most children, or at least children back then, could sense a change in their parents for whatever reason. My mother was a simple, good woman. She was totally devoted to my father. Although younger by a few years than my dad, he was her whole life, just as we children were. It became obvious a few days later that what had been on my parents' minds was how they would deal with 'Operation Pied Piper'. I suppose that is when I felt that my life truly began and will always be at the forefront of my memory - the evacuation.

Chapter 2

The Platform to Hatch Beauchamp

Two years prior to the start of World War II, the British government had begun planning for a possible massive evacuation of London and other major cities. If indeed war came, the great cities of England would become potential targets of bomb attacks. The reasoning behind this plan was, with the advent of a powerful German Air Force, most experts anticipated tens of thousands of dead as a result of raids.

In September of 1939, these fears were realized when the invading German Armed Forces virtually wiped out Warsaw and other Polish cities. After witnessing this unprecedented destruction, Britain laid the ground work of what would be known as Operation Pied Piper. The architect of the plan was Sir John Anderson, also known for being instrumental in the development of the Anderson Shelter.

My mother's story began when she boarded the train at Plaistow Station which took her to the market town of Taunton, in the West Country. From there, a number of Evacuees were sent to the village of Hatch Beauchamp. Within Hatch Beauchamp was a manor house known as Hatch Court. She was to spend the next 6 years at 'The Court', as it was known among the locals.

The children of Operation Pied Piper were evacuated to countless towns and villages across Britain at the start of the Second World War. In those grim times of September 1939, 3.5 million children were relocated in the largest single movement of people in the history of Great Britain. Amazingly, it took place in just over four days. My mother, two uncles, and aunt were among those children who were taken from their parents and moved to safety.

The 2005 book 'Out of Harm's Way', by Jessica Mann, tells the stories of those children who left England and went to locations all over the world to escape the war. Many of them had tragic lives and some died from the experience. There is a misconception that the wealthy sent their children abroad to escape the war in England, as Ms Mann so expertly explains in her book, this was not the case. A parent will do anything to keep their children from harm, but their efforts were unfortunately not always successful. While my mother and her brothers and sister did not leave England, they were never out of harm's way, nor were millions of other babies and children of the Blitz. But she survived and embarked on a life that would take her from the East End of London to the countryside, where she would experience so many different events in the war years.

During the middle of August 1939, members of the London County Council came around to homes in the East End and throughout London, to find out how many children were in each house and how many would need to be evacuated in the event of war. Unknown to my mother, her parents had been informed of the possibility of a massive evacuation and had decided against telling the four children. As a result of the government's plans, my grandmother silently prepared for the possibility of her children being taken away from her and my grandfather. The reality came with a knock on the door, warning all parents that the children were to leave the day war was declared. As there seemed no hope for peace with Germany, the plan was to prepare all children for evacuation, by train, for an initial period of two weeks, according to government orders.

The year was 1939. I remember the date well, August 31st 1939. I was 12 years old, my little sister Marie was 9 and my twin brothers, Charles and Dennis, were 5. We were notified by the London County Council to be at Burks School in Plaistow, in the East End of London at 8.30 the following morning. We were to be ready to be evacuated and taken to places in the countryside, along with thousands of other London children. Where exactly in the countryside was not disclosed to the parents or their children. This was known as Operation Pied Piper. War was imminent. We had no idea at that young age how our lives would change.

We were at school a few days before war was declared when our teacher told the girls in my class to pick up a can of tinned beef, biscuits, and barley sugar to take home with us at the end of the day. We were instructed to give it to our parents. I did not know why, but I did as I was told and took the three items to my mother. She took them from me silently and put them in the larder.

On the evening of August 31st we were all at home, it was also my father's day off from his job and he sat listening to the radio after dinner. My mother was in the kitchen putting away the dinner plates with Marie and me helping her. As Charles and Dennis played on the floor with their toys, talking as little boys do, my dad suddenly told everyone to be quiet. The radio was, as usual, tuned to the news programme of the BBC. As we all sat silently, the announcer said all children in London were to assemble at their local school the following morning. They were to be escorted by their parents to assembly areas for transportation out of the city.

As I looked at my mother in the kitchen, she stared ahead with tears welling up in her eyes. My father sat in the lounge looking at the radio expressionless. Even though I was only twelve, I knew something was terribly wrong. As the silence overtook all of us in the room, my mother said quietly, "Children, gather up a change of clothes and bring them to me, you are leaving in the morning for a trip to the country." Almost immediately Marie, Charles, and Dennis began to ask why they had to leave and started to cry. Usually my father would tell us to be quiet and do what my mother said, but this night he sat in his chair and said nothing. I went to my mother and said, "Why must we leave?" She said, "Eileen, all the children in the neighbourhood are leaving in the morning. Please do as I say, you won't be gone long. You must get your things together, help the little ones and don't ask questions." It was then I began to cry uncontrollably. We were not allowed to take any toys or personal items, only clothes, gas masks, food which the school had given us and our identity cards. I begged her not to make us go. She broke down and she began to cry as well. As my father tried to calm all of us, I could tell he was struggling to maintain his composure. I did not even know what the word composure meant but I knew my father never cried, and that night he was upset, more upset than I had ever seen him.

As the night wore on and my mother prepared our clothes and placed them neatly folded into cloth sacks (we had no suitcases) my brothers and sister began to grow hysterical. They cried constantly and kept saying they would not go. My father softly but sternly told us we must go and we would return shortly. We needed to think of this as an adventure in the country. I remember no-one slept. My parents busied themselves, held us to comfort us, and then, one by one, we all fell asleep for a short time, soon to wake up and the crying to start all over again. Looking back it must have been heart wrenching for my parents to know their children were to leave in the morning. They did not know where we were going, how long we would be gone, or when we would return. One thing I clearly remember is my father constantly getting up and picking up all of us, holding us and telling us things would be all right. Even today, in my mind, I can almost smell his pipe tobacco; it has always stayed with me. Without exception it was one of the most terrible nights of my entire life.

What my mother did not know at the time was that this was the last night of peace and one of the last nights they would all be together as a family. My mother found out later from her Aunt Lucy, that her mother had told the Council member, who came to the house that August, that she would not part with her children. She had said if war came and the city was bombed her family would stay together and if necessary die together. Her mother and father made the choice they would not let their children be taken from them. Unfortunately, when war did come, the choice was not theirs to make. They had no family in the countryside of Great Britain, they did not have the means to send the children to Canada or America, they were poor, their options few and they would in the end send their children with the other evacuees to where they would have a modicum of safety, the countryside.

Before dawn, we were all awake and as my mother prepared tea for my father and a bowl of oats for all of us, tears streamed down her cheeks, my father walked aimlessly from one room to another, constantly stopping to pick up my brothers and hold them, amidst the constant crying of the four of us children. About 7.30am we gathered up our belongings and walked outside to the street. Libra Road was full of people. Almost everyone was crying, grownups and children alike. There was no traffic of any kind that cool, bright morning; no buses, no milk wagons, no cars; everything had been moved to the side of the road to allow all of us children a clear path to the train station. If the day had not been so terrible, it would have been a great day for a street party. The weather was perfect. The only sound that I remember was children crying, and parents walking beside them crying as well. Everyone moved slowly, but orderly to the school yard.

Once there, we lined up in rows behind the school standard, where the police surrounded the playground, not allowing the parents past the gates. When we were all counted, we were marched in single file for the 2 mile journey to Plaistow Station. My mother and many other mothers, walked alongside us, begging the police for information as to where we were being taken. They refused to answer any questions, because they were informed by the local government not to tell our whereabouts for our own safety. As we arrived at the station platforms, all traffic was still at a standstill. Nothing was to go in or out of the station until all evacuees were out of London.

My mother told me, when the children started the walk from the school yard to the train station, she looked across the street and saw her father; he seemed to have a faraway look. As she walked by he just stared at them. Her mother, as were all the mothers that day, seemed inconsolable in her grief. As the children moved to the trains, the only sound that rose above the crying of the children, were the sounds coming from the trains. Like sinister steel monsters, steam hissed from the engines, and the coaches waited in silence for the little children to get on board. My mother and hundreds of other children, crying, kicking, screaming, and bewildered, got on trains that would take them from their parents and the lives they had known. From that late August day in 1939 life would never be the same again for any of them.

We boarded the trains and were packed into very tight spaces. It was very hot and everyone was crying. My sister was so upset she became ill and vomited constantly. I did everything I could to help her. My father had given me strict orders before leaving, that, "On no account, are the four of you to be separated." One of my last memories of my dad that day was of him with his head in his hands, weeping. It was the first time I ever saw my dad cry.

The London Underground carried us non-stop to Paddington Station. Trains had been given special clearance to be waved through by station attendants. They were marked with codes, so they would arrive at their final destination non-stop. The idea was that evacuees might get off the train if it was to stop. Once at Paddington Station we disembarked, and then boarded a steam train that went non-stop to Taunton, a town in the West Country of England, 150 miles from London.

When we arrived at the Taunton station, we were marched to a field and told to sit in rows while officials lined up buses to take us to surrounding villages where we would be billeted, to a place that would become our home for a long time. While I sat with Marie, Dennis and Charles, a strange feeling came over me and told me to get up and move over with another group of children. As I moved my sister and brothers *over to another group, I was in fact disobeying orders given to us by the authorities to sit still. But we moved anyway and no one seemed to notice. That strange feeling told me again to just sit and wait. With our new group, we then boarded a bus and drove 6 miles to a village called Hatch Beauchamp. It was our first trip to the countryside outside London.*

Whilst the departure of all the children took several days to complete, parents were not allowed on station platforms. There are many pictures of British mothers running down platforms at stations, screaming to their children, who were heading to destinations unknown to their parents, and to stay with people they didn't know. It was several weeks until parents were finally allowed to visit their children. (Those who billeted the evacuees were to be paid by the Government a weekly allowance of 8 shillings and 6 pence or 42 pence in today's money. The parents of the evacuees were to match that).

    Once in Taunton, after an endless day of being shunted from one location to another, my mother, her sister, and twin brothers saw Hatch Beauchamp and Hatch Court for the first time. It was, and remains to this day, an imposing home.

While this was a very sad day for me, it was also very exciting. We were Londoners and had never been to a 'typical' English village before, where there was a post-office, village shop and a blacksmith's forge. Everyone was quite scared as we filed into the village hall and then sat down whilst the billeting officer and a group of villagers looked us over. I can't remember just how many people were there, but I saw this lady wearing a grey suit with a red, white and beige knitted top, brown and white shoes and grey hair, and she seemed to have a very kind face. As I sat and watched her, I finally got up and approached her and said, "My Dad said my family cannot be separated. There are four of us." She then instructed the four of us to sit over to the side and proceeded to pick seven other children. They were also brothers and sisters and a little boy that was in our care. Their names were Grace and Reggie Cutteram, Rose and Stanley Keely, Julia, Tubby and Sidney Pinder. The 11 of us ranged in age from 5 to 13 years and were all from East London.

The rest of the evacuees that were taken to the same little village were from North London.

This lady, who had picked the 11 of us wide-eyed children, was Mrs Andrew Hamilton Gault of Hatch Court in Hatch Beauchamp. She was considered by many locals as 'the Lady of the village'. She took us outside where there were two cars; a huge green Bentley driven by a chauffeur in full uniform, named Durman, and a Rolls Royce driven by a very tall and handsome man, Brigadier Gault. We got into the cars and proceeded through the village until we reached two enormous iron gates. They led to a long driveway, which wound round into a huge courtyard, where a full company of servants, in all sorts of uniforms, were waiting for us. Hatch had 10 servants at the start of the war. As I laid eyes on the house for the first time, I saw then, as now, a most imposing home. I had to ask myself "What is this place called Hatch Court?"

Hatch Court 1940

Marie, Charles, Dennis and Eileen – 1939

Mrs Gault and 11 Evacuees

Chapter 3

The Manor House and a New Home

The history of Hatch Beauchamp can be traced back to 1092 in Saxon times. The village was under the control of Robert of Beauchamp, a loyal ally of William the Conqueror. Around 1300 it was known as a market place for local trading, but this has long since vanished. The village, in 1939, remained much as it had for centuries, small, quiet, and dominated by two large homes; Hatch Park and Hatch Court. Hatch Court was built around 1755, in the Palladian architectural style. Prior to the building of Hatch Court, a great house from the Middle Ages had existed on the site, but had fallen into ruin during the 17th century.

Thomas Prowse had the house built for John Collins in 1755. (Hatch Court has a long and varied history, which can be found in 'Hatch Court, Images of England', various copies of Country Life, English Heritage or Hatch Beauchamp Church, Hatch Beauchamp,
www.weavo.co.uk.hatch/hatch.htm).
Today, Hatch Court is privately owned by Mr Philip Gibbs and his wife, Melanie, who have undertaken many renovations since purchasing the estate.

The Church of St John the Baptist sits directly behind the house and is still used for services today by the villagers. Eileen's sister, Marie Barnett, is buried there and rests some fifty feet from the cemetery's most renowned grave, John (later Lord) Chard, who as a Lieutenant, was awarded the Victoria Cross (the equivalent to the United States Congressional Medal of Honor) for his part in the defence of Rorke's Drift in the Anglo-Zulu War of 1879.

In the 1920s, Andrew Hamilton Gault of Montreal, Canada, purchased the home for his wife, Dorothy. Gault was no ordinary landowner. He was from one of Canada's richest families who had made a fortune in lumber, in Canada, during the late 1800s and early 1900s. But what made Hamilton Gault so distinctive and such a renowned landowner, in Hatch Beauchamp, was his military accomplishments. In the First World War, Gault DSO, ED,CD, with his own money equipped and financed a military regiment (the Empire's last privately raised regiment, and by all accounts the last privately funded regiment in any country's military) to fight for Canada in the service of the British Empire.

The regiment as it became known is 'The Princess Patricia's Canadian Light Infantry'. The regiment won numerous battles honours in WWI, and became legendary at the Battle of Freezenburg. Gault was wounded numerous times and, while acting as Brigade Major, refused to be evacuated until the end of the day, when his men were moved to the rear and properly cared for. (Jeffery Williams has written an excellent history of the regiment called 'First in the Field'. For those who want to learn more this is a highly recommended resource, along with 'Once a Patricia' by C. Sidney Frost). The regiment saw action in both World Wars, and was the first Allied Force to enter Amsterdam in early 1945. They also served in Korea, the Gulf wars and Afghanistan. They remain to this day a part of the permanent Canadian Defense Force.

However, Gault also served as a member of Parliament, representing Taunton, beginning in 1925 and remained a member representing his constituency until 1934, when he announced his retirement. Later in his illustrious life he was honoured by the United States, Canada, England, and the Princess Pat's for his contributions to the soldiers of the regiment and his work in both World Wars.

This is the home and life my mother entered in 1939. To leave the hard life and working class of the East End and begin a life in a Georgian Mansion built in the mid 1700s, owned by a famous Canadian General (he was promoted to Brigadier in 1942), was, to say the least, a cultural shock and major lifestyle change for a London girl of twelve and her brothers and sister.

In order to gain an appreciation for Hatch Court and its part in this story you must think back to the England of the 1930s. There was the upper class and the lower class of people, there was no true middle class, as we know it today. People quite frankly were considered wealthy or they were considered workers. My mother, who came from what would be truly considered "a working class family", had just arrived into the class of people who were then considered wealthy. I have visited Hatch Court numerous times over the years. I was married in 1987, at the Church of St. John the Baptist, behind Hatch. At that time, the owners, Commander and Mrs Barry Nation, were so gracious and allowed my wife and I to have our reception in Hatch Court, because they had known my mother during the war and were friends of my late Aunt, Marie, who at that time lived in Hatch Beauchamp on the grounds of what was during the war, property of Hatch Court.

For me it was like stepping back in time. I could only imagine the grandeur and splendour that Hatch Court once was and the impression it must have made on my mother those many years ago. However, along with the house and the life it reflected, what made it so different for my mother, were the people who regularly visited the 'Court' to see the Brigadier and Mrs Gault.

The Gaults were part of the 'Gentry' of Hatch Beauchamp and lived in this large manor house, with over 700 acres of farmland and forest. They employed 10 servants when war broke out in 1939 and their cars consisted of a Bentley and a Rolls Royce, not the type of transportation my mother and her family were used to riding in. Neither was she accustomed to meeting the many important and distinguished guests who frequented The Court throughout her stay.

As the late summer turned to autumn, the village took on a feeling of settling in for the evacuees and the locals. There can be no doubt that Eileen and her fellow evacuees were very fortunate in being billeted with the Gaults. Many other children, were simply dropped on the doorsteps of thousands of homes throughout rural Britain and were frequently treated as outsiders and felt unwanted. Some were mistreated, or forced to do very menial tasks for little or no reward. There is even evidence of physical and sexual assault.

It was not like that here, however, as Eileen describes in her impressions of Mrs Gault, the servants and Hatch Court, *the biggest house I had ever seen up close.*

When we stepped out of the cars, we were taken to our rooms which were over the kitchens and under a huge clock, known as the Clock Tower. The boys were put in one room and the girls in another. Each one of us was provided with a camp bed. There was a third room that was reserved for the teacher, or whoever was in charge of looking after us. (Miss Ames, a teacher from St James Norlands School in North London was there for a short while to help us settle in.)

After we had put our belongings away, we walked to the mess hall for tea. We had to go downstairs, out of the side door, along the path, through a passage and across the courtyard. The room was huge with flagstone floors, tall windows with shutters and two long tables. The tables were set with enamel mugs and plates. There was a smaller table with toys on it. A lady sat at the end of the table and told us we were at Hatch Court in Hatch Beauchamp, Taunton in Somerset. The house belonged to Brigadier and Mrs Andrew Hamilton Gault. As I sat there, listening to her, I was wondering how we all came to arrive in Hatch. I still think it was an act of God. We were the only group of brothers and sisters who were not separated and sent to different billets.

We were all so confused and frightened. The little boys were crying and just wanted to go home. Grace, Rose, Marie and I tried our best to comfort them. We took them back to their rooms and put them into bed amid the sobbing. It was after all, a very upsetting day. For me, and I am sure the rest of the children of Operation Pied Piper, August 31, 1939 was our "longest day."

Mrs Gault 1940

Marie and Charles with the village children

Chapter 4

"Getting on with it"

From shortly after we arrived, our food was put on a table outside the kitchen window. The scullery maid would call us and we would run across the courtyard and take it back to the mess hall, where it was dished out to the rest of the children. After we had finished our meals, the four girls would wash the dishes in the big tubs in the bake house across the courtyard. We also did the washing for all 11 children in the tubs in the bake house and hung the clothes on the clothes line in the courtyard.

There was an Episcopal nun named Sister Phoebe, from St. James, that came for a few weeks to take care of us. She used to take us for long walks. On September 3rd, she took us to church and told us that war had been declared at 11.00am that Sunday morning. We sang "Oh God Our Help in Ages Past." We always sang that during war time. We girls cried because we knew our parents were in danger in London, but we knew the air-raid shelters had been dug in the gardens and that barrage balloons were flying over London to keep the German bombers from flying low....but we still cried.

Our parents, at that time, still did not know where we were, but Brigadier Gault told us he would write to each one and tell them we were together at his house. Mrs Gault was kind to us and so were most of the servants, but no-one actually took care of us. We took care of ourselves and it was up to the four girls to take care of the little ones. Mrs Gault would come into the mess room dressed in her beautiful evening clothes, just before it was time to have her dinner in the "front" of the house. Dinner was always served by Mills, the butler, and Frank, the footman. Beautiful silver serving dishes were used and beautiful food was cooked and prepared by Mrs Hoare, the cook, Betty, the kitchen maid, and Evelyn, the scullery maid.

We had been at Hatch Court two weeks when the government allowed our parents to come and visit us. My mother came down on the bus on Friday, and stayed with Mrs Pinkham in the village. Mrs Pinkham was a local village lady who allowed mothers of some of the village 'evacs' to stay at her home when they visited their children. She was a wonderful lady. We were so very happy to see our mother. She brought Marie and me new dresses and shoes and the boys new clothes. It was such heartbreak on Sunday when she had to go back to London.

The evacuees went to the village school, in the beginning, for just half a day. The village children would stand and look at us like we were from another world, but we were Londoners and walked proudly past them. We girls in our gym-slips and blouses, which were our uniforms, thought the country kids were stupid and, to be frank, some of them were. There was absolutely no comparison as far as education went. Firstly it was a one room school, and we thought that was silly compared to our big London schools. We did this for about two weeks, then Miss Ames, a teacher from London, managed to get the village hall for us and we had regular school days from 9-4. As much as I didn't like her, she was an excellent teacher. The floor boards were about half an inch apart and the wind would scream into the room. So in the morning, she would take us for a long walk to get warmed up before our first lesson. We had proper books and did wonderful country dancing, singing, and sewing and even learned the national anthems of every country that was on our side in the war. It seemed to me to be a few years later before we learned the United States national anthem. I felt that, as it sounded exactly like our national anthem, the Americans were not very original, but at least they had good taste.

So our days were busy going to school. When we went home for lunch, we had to walk up Curry Mallet Road and up the back drive, in case the German airmen might be flying around, for we would be in danger of being machine-gunned. They were known to do that in the day time. As we walked home from school we used to sing all the war songs, it kept our spirits up and helped the little boys take their mind off being away from home.

Night time though was always the worst time. We girls would take the little boys upstairs and bathe them and put them to bed. Charles would always cry. He would have nightmares and cry out of the window "I've got pictures in my eyes."

Then he would call Marie and she would go up and lie beside him until he went to sleep.

After we put the little ones to bed, Grace, Rose, Marie and I would be in that huge mess hall and we would put on little skits, anything to amuse ourselves until it was time to go to bed. Sometimes Evelyn would come over and sing to us and recite poetry. We really loved her as she did her best to make our lives a little happier. She had beautiful long black hair and always had some sort of props to use, like a scarf around her to become an 'Indian Maiden' and sing Red River Valley, or else put a red rose in her hair and recite 'The Highwayman' to us.

Every Tuesday night, Mrs Saunders, at the Methodist Chapel, would run a magic lantern for all the evacuees. We could go and Evelyn used to come with us. Some of the older boys from North London used to follow us home and Grace, Rose and I had sort of boyfriends. We played in the long evenings outside on the lawn or in the park. We could play anywhere, as long as it wasn't in front of the dining room window, where 'The family' would be having dinner.

When I remember our instructions on how to behave, from the head housemaid, Rogers, and how we were not to play in front of the dining room windows, while the family (Gaults and their guests) were eating, a part of me still resents her 'orders'. It was as if we would distract them from their meals, which were certainly of a higher quality than ours, most days. I could always feel my face redden and my hands instinctively turned into a fist, when she ushered us away from the front yard, and sent us to the Courtyard by the stables and garages to clean up before she allowed us into the servants' hall to eat. There was never enough to eat for all of us, everything was rationed.

At first people were told rationing would just be on a few essential items. In January 1940 the Government rationed butter, ham, bacon and sugar. That was soon followed, in March, by all meats. Little by little almost all foodstuffs were rationed and there was little left that would not require coupons to obtain. Eventually, everything was rationed, or impossible to find if it wasn't. Items such as tea (a British staple), margarine, cheese, etc… and then in June 1941, clothes were rationed and subject to coupons. In December 1941 a government programme came into being that established a points system for all canned and processed foods. By July 1942 all goods were severely rationed, as food and essentials were running short, and priority was given to the soldiers, sailors, and airmen who were fighting all over the world. My mother has forgotten exactly when soap was rationed, but she remembered it did not seem to affect the little boys, including her brothers, too much, as they were not too fond of bath time at any time.

We knew that Mrs Gault did her best to help with the shortages that the children experienced. But as young children, the cruelest blow of all came, in July of 1942, when all chocolates and sweets were put on the ration list. To us, as with any child, chocolate and sweets were viewed as a special treat. I remember my brother Dennis saying he was really mad at the Germans now. He blamed them personally for the lack of his favourite chocolate, Cadbury's!

My mother has often told me of ration books, points, weekly or monthly allocations, for what we would consider everyday items. They were, however, always reminded that many children in other parts of the world had nothing to eat at all, much less than worrying about a piece of Cadbury's chocolate. By 1942 she was 16, and while she always said, *"You adjusted to shortages, but people of all ages grew tired of "making do" or being told there's a war on."* She said that along with everything else, women's cosmetics were rationed, because many of the ingredients were used in the making of war materials, and by 1942 all cosmetics were in short supply and you were lucky if you could find any at all.

If you could find cosmetics you were indeed fortunate. As the rationing became more severe, the Government launched, what many thought was a ridiculous programme, called "Put your best face forward". While posters and people on the BBC radio programmes talked about how "Good looks and good morale went hand in hand", it was absurd to worry about looking your best when you had not had a decent meal in months or longer. Besides, getting cosmetics was next to impossible unless you had a decent job, knew someone who actually had cosmetics, or dealt in the black market (there was not a large cosmetic black market operating in Hatch Beauchamp as best I can remember). Right, put your best face forward, what a joke! In time, I was to discover that the ladies who visited The Court and spent time with the Brigadier and Mrs Gault, sometimes, but not always, were sympathetic to the fact that the few teenage girls in the house lacked the ability to "Put our best Face Forward." It took some creativity and sad faces on my part, but from time to time, I did get the occasional bar of Yardley soap, nail varnish, or the most coveted item of all - perfume.

I was also fortunate that Mrs Gault's niece, Anne Sykes, (many years later, the owner of Hatch Court) and some of her friends who worked in Taunton, would stay at Hatch on some weekends. She would from time to time give us some make-up, rouge, and other bits of what we thought were essentials to looking grown up.

With the complicated system of rationing imposed by the wartime government, my mother remembered food was always higher on the list of importance than make-up. She also said, when the Americans arrived, in 1943, some of the girls in Hatch and the surrounding villages, took on the attitude that perhaps being well made up might be as important as food. She recalled that while everyone had to make do with whatever was available and ration cards were like gold, you still had to make wise use of what you had. If her parents had not sent packages of necessities for her and her brothers and sister things would have been much grimmer. As the war dragged on things would nonetheless, seem grim indeed.

Hatch Beauchamp School

Chapter 5

"Our First Christmas - 1939"

Christmas seemed to be quickly coming upon us. At our first Christmas in 1939, we had a wonderful Christmas Tableau. We did wonderful plays and dancing. We advertised it through the different villages by going to Ilminster, Isle Abbots, Merryfield and West Hatch, putting up handmade posters in the local shops and church entrances. We charged a small admittance fee. The village hall was packed with standing room only. I was the Arch Angel Gabriel. Marie was also an angel, and Dennis and Charles were shepherds and elves in the other play. The villagers loved it and gave us a standing ovation. They had never seen anything like it. We were so proud of ourselves and our teacher.

With some of the money we had collected, we bought knitting wool of several colours, khaki, Air Force blue and navy blue. All of us girls knitted gloves, mittens, socks and hats. With any money left over, we lined up at the different local stores and bought soap and combs and put them in the same packages of knitted items we prepared to send to different regiments, Airforce stations and the Navy. (We did this for the various regiments throughout the war). It gave us all a sense of worth that we were able to give something to the war effort.

Just before Christmas it began to snow. The Brigadier and Mrs Gault summoned all the children to the front steps outside, we didn't know why. The Brigadier had the groom saddle up two of their horses, Daffodil and Butterfly and the Brigadier rode one and Mrs Gault rode the other. They then told us 11 children to follow the woodsmen, Napper and Faulkner, into the woods. To our surprise, we were asked to help select the Christmas tree for the house. After we had selected one, we watched the woodsmen cut it down and we all helped pull it back to the house.

I was not sure if we would have a Christmas celebration or not. But just in case, I wrote to my mother to ask her to send me my best dress. I had been a bridesmaid the year before to Beatie and Cyril Rozee, (my aunt and uncle who I was very close to) and I just loved that dress. It had a long pink skirt and short sleeves with tiny pink roses on the top. I also had her send me my silver shoes. If we did happen to have a party, I wanted to look my best.

A week before Christmas, Marie, Dennis, Charles and I received four huge boxes from our mother and father. I got my bridesmaid dress and silver shoes, along with a brand new red velvet dress. Marie got a green velvet dress because of her red hair and the boys got new navy blue coats. What a grand surprise.

I had begun to notice that many uniformed men were arriving at The Court. Since the Brigadier was still a Colonel in the Princess Patricia's Canadian Light Infantry, which was now stationed in Aldershot, quite a few officers began arriving to spend leave. With all the excitement going on, I was sure there was going to be a party. But still nothing was said to us.

As Christmas Eve approached, we were told we would have a lovely Christmas dinner on Christmas Day. On Christmas Eve, Mrs Gault and her niece, Ann, placed gifts at the foot of each of our 11 beds, so each of us would have something to open. I look back and think of what their kind act meant to all of us that first Christmas. When we awoke on Christmas Day we opened them. We got pyjamas, gloves and socks. Then we were told to be ready for Christmas dinner at noon.

We all got dressed up (me in my pink dress, silver shoes and Marie in her new green velvet dress) and went into the servants' hall along with all the servants. There, laid out on long tables, was turkey, ham, Christmas pudding, mince pies and all the trimmings. What a wonderful sight! It was just marvellous. We all enjoyed it so much.

Then that afternoon, Mrs Gault invited all of us evacuees and the village children into the house, in the Long Room for afternoon tea. As we entered the Long Room, we saw the tree we had selected, for the first time since we had carried it back to the house. It was so beautifully decorated with an angel on top. There were records playing music and tables filled with wonderful things to eat, and there was a huge fire burning in the fireplace, as it was still snowing outside. Brigadier Gault played Santa Claus. All the children received gifts of candy, diaries for the girls, writing pads, pencils and long woollen underwear. All of us, the 11 evacuees, had bought gifts that we could afford for the Brigadier. We had all bought ashtrays. My sister Marie had dropped hers and it had shattered. She was absolutely devastated that she had nothing to give him. Our teacher, Miss Ames, rushed Marie down to the Post Office where she bought a handkerchief for a sixpence. The Brigadier, having heard this, opened her gift and stood up and said, "This is the most beautiful handkerchief I have ever received." He then proceeded to show it to everyone. Marie just beamed in delight. This was a typical example of just how remarkable the Brigadier was.

There were lots of soldiers and friends of the Gaults attending. What a lovely crowd to behold. As the records continued to play, people began dancing and having sing-songs. Oh, what a lovely day it was!

It was truly a child's Christmas dream. It was also very sad that we did not have our parents there to share it with us. The war quickly crept back into my mind and I so missed all of our family being together to share this special time. Maybe, just maybe, we could go back home soon. I could not know that we would never have a family Christmas again with my parents. So many thousands of children like us would experience the same fate. Family Christmases, like those before the war, would become only memories. But, in a way, we were fortunate. At least, we children we were always together at Christmas during those years. Many families who were separated were never reunited.

Soon, reality set in again and, after our Christmas holiday, we went back to school. By this time our lives were pretty much routine. We always kept up with the goings on of the war. Our teacher was very clever and also taught us so many wonderful things like poetry, plays, sewing, knitting and literature. She managed (I don't know how) to get the best of everything for us.

London Blitz

Chapter 6

"Return to London – Hell from the Skies"
The Blitz

Spring came and we enjoyed seeing all the lambs being born, and we would go up into the woods and pick bluebells, wild violets and daffodils and gorgeous primroses. We would line boxes with ferns and put the flowers in them to send to our parents in London.

Time began to hang heavily and, since there had been no air-raids on London, some of the children had gone home and I wanted to go back to London too. My mother came down in August 1940 and took us back home on the bus. We were to go home for six weeks. My father met us at the bus station and as we were walking home, I heard him say to my mother, "They were over last night and hit the Becton gas works." I knew what he meant, but Marie and the twins were so excited to be home they never knew.

A week went by and we loved being at home with our parents again and seeing all the old neighbours. Grace Hill came to my house and wanted to take me to see a friend who lived on Barking Road. It was Saturday, Sept 7th.

Although the war had begun a little over a year before, thus far London had been spared German bombs. The Luftwaffe had chosen to attack British airfields and radar stations, a strategy which they did not know was working. However, London itself had not experienced the terror that had laid waste to cities such as Warsaw, Rotterdam, Cracow and countless other cities and villages on the European continent; until now.

The Blitz began on Saturday September 7, 1940. My mother remembers it like it was yesterday, having just returned home from the West Country. France had surrendered and now England stood truly alone. All of Great Britain had known the war was coming to their island and the people of London knew they would be a major target. However, they had no idea what awaited them. In the East End, home of many working Londoners, those who would be in the thick of whatever happened, waited. On the day of the 'first official night of the Blitz' the sirens began to wail shortly before dusk. My mother said her father simply told the family that they should prepare for the worst and see what the Hun would do. He always referred to the Germans as Huns ever since he had fought in the First World War.

As darkness began to envelop London, the faint rumbling of aircraft engines slowly grew to a roar. The far off specks in the clear September sky began to take the shape of planes. And not just any planes, Heinkel He-111s and Dornier DO-17s bombers. After 70 years, my mother still recalls the name and makes of the planes over England that night. I guess it is something you never forget even after all those years. The German Luftwaffe had arrived for the first of many terrible nights that would turn the shabby dock areas and the East End into a real life nightmare. The Blitz had started and for the people on the streets far below who stared transfixed at the oncoming planes, hell had arrived.

The evening of September 7 1940, would be the first of 57 continuous nights of air-raids, during which over 5300 tons of bombs would wreak havoc on the world's largest city and the first of over 147,000 Londoners (2,000 were to die on the first night alone) would pay with their lives, as the horror of war struck home with a vengeance. Just after 8.00pm waves of planes came towards London and they kept up the bombing until 4.30 the next morning. The German bombers followed the winding River Thames and were able to bomb at will due to the smoke and flames rising from the docklands.

According to Peter Fleming's 1957 book, 'Invasion 1940', the night of September 7, brought destruction on a scale that far surpassed even the recollections of those who lived through that night.

Between five and six o'clock on the evening of Saturday, 7 September, some 320 German bombers, supported by over 600 fighters, flew up the Thames and proceeded to bomb Woolwich Arsenal, Beckton Gas Works, Westminster and Kensington. They succeeded in causing a serious fire in the docks, an area of about 1½ square miles between North Woolwich Road and the Thames were almost destroyed, and the population of Silvertown was surrounded by fire and had to be evacuated by water.

The London docks were now a raging inferno. Barrels of rum exploded, paint drums went up in flames and melting rubber from the docks sent smoke thousands of feet into the night sky. While fire-boats moved up and down the Thames to try to quell the inferno, they were fighting a losing battle. Burning sugar from the huge Tate and Lyle Factory flowed into the river Thames, forcing the fire-boats away from the blaze.

My grandfather was trapped in this terror and recalled later that he was sure that he was going to be killed, as there was nowhere to run to for safety for him and his mates. The East End, then a jumble of docks and warehouses, burned so brightly that the fires could be seen 30 miles away in Ilford, Essex, (where my Aunt lives to this day).

When we arrived at this friend's house, I suddenly had a strange feeling of doom and asked the lady if she had an air-raid shelter. She laughed and said no. I jumped up and wanted to leave at once, which we did. But I insisted on going through Ballam St. Park where I knew there were underground shelters and barrage balloon stations.

As we were walking through the park, we saw Mr Pinder, whose little boy had been evacuated with us, but had since returned home. Mr Pinder took us back to his house and we no sooner got there than the sirens blew and we all went into the Anderson Shelter in the back yard.

The 'Battle of Britain' had begun. I looked out at the sky only to see squadrons of German planes. The throbbing sound 'For you - For you' that came from their engines was almost deafening as they flew up the Thames and branched out, ready to drop their bombs. We could see them coming down with their attack guns blazing. It was terrible.

We waited until the all clear sounded and then ran home to Libra Road. My poor mother was running down the street looking for me. People were in the streets, standing outside what were once their homes, running along the roads with their belongings in prams and their children in tow. I thought the world had come to an end and really the world I had known, had.

The next morning, Sunday, my mother spent the whole day taking mattresses and blankets and getting the shelter ready for what was to become our almost permanent home. The days wore into nights. Early one evening I was standing at my front door when Bill Miller, a young man two houses down said, "There's the siren, get into the shelter". My mum and dad had just gone out for the evening and they came running back into the house. Mum grabbed a torch and we went into this corrugated hole in the ground, little did we know we would not come out until morning. It was a terrible night. So many of the bombs being dropped were delayed-action and as the firemen were fighting the fires, these bombs would explode, killing civilians and the brave firemen alike.

During those first six weeks of the London Blitz, if you can imagine, six people were living in a 6' x 6' tin shell dug into the ground. Dirt covered the top of it and it had garbage can lids tied together and propped up for the door.

When the sirens blew, sometimes as early as 6pm, that tin shell would be sealed and no one moved until the all-clear was sounded. I can still remember looking up at the ceiling, watching the condensation forming and it glistening in my mother's flashlight. You could see a drip, drip, drip, as the condensation ran down the sides onto to the wooden floor, like tiny rain drops. My dad had put down a wooden floor before the mattress was carried into the shelter, so that the four of us kids could lie down. I can't ever remember my mum or dad lying down. They just sat, either side of the door, watching, waiting and listening. We heard the screams of the Stuka dive-bombers, the terrible scream of the bombs falling through the air and the explosions. Hour after hour the incendiary bombs, which fell in packs, turned the night sky blood red. The sky was so bright you could read a newspaper by the light from the fires. London was ablaze.

Around 4.00 on most evenings, people would be walking along the streets with little bundles under their arms going to the shelters in the parks. People would have 'premonitions' and think they would be safer there. They would also go to St. Anthony's Church because they felt safe. One night my mum got us ready to go there, but my Dad said, 'No, we were given the air raid shelters and that's where we are going to stay.' St. Anthony's was hit that night by a bomb and many people were killed. Apart from the terrible noise of the bombers, the noise from the Ack-Ack guns firing at them was unbelievable. Some of these guns were from ships of the Royal Navy. They were mounted on trucks and soldiers would run them through the streets firing all the time. They hoped the German pilots would think we had lots of guns, when really we had very few to cover the whole of London.

There was no-one to help us; our survival depended on the brave young men of the Royal Air Force. These men, in their late teens and early twenties, flew Spitfires and Hurricanes from Biggin Hill, North Weald, Hornchurch, Henley and other airfields around London and Kent. Sometimes they slept on the ground by their planes. These brave men, vastly outnumbered, were trying to stop the hundreds of bombers reaching London. They will always be known as the 'The Few', so called by Sir Winston Churchill in his speech, "Never in the field of human conflict, has so much been owed by so many to so few."

No-one ever complained, but we all knew the fate of Britain, Europe and much of the World hung on the shoulders of the 'Few' and the brave British people.

My mother, her family, and their neighbours rushed to the Underground on the nights she recalls the bombing became unusually intense. Her parents thought September 7 was to be the first of many nights they would gather up the children and seek safety. My mother always thought that one night they would change from a family of terrified people to a family of victims. The feeling and fear still remains with her 70 years later.

As people they knew were killed, their neighbours, school chums, the people down at the end of Libra Road, their terror grew and they did what they could to escape death. While I cannot begin to know their fear, I gather my mother felt each night brought them closer to becoming a statistic.

But, they did not and could not reach the local Underground station every night. On some nights they and many others were turned away as the local station would quickly fill to capacity and the Air Raid Warden would quietly, and with sadness in his voice, tell my grandmother "Sorry love, no more room".

It was then, my mother, grandfather, grandmother, uncles and aunt would utilize their last option. They would take blankets, a torch (flashlight), a few scraps of food, a toy or two for the children and go into their backyard to a cramped, musty, damp smelling hole in the backyard known as an 'Anderson Shelter'.

My mother's shelter was no different from thousands of others. A hole was dug, a piece of steel or corrugated metal was placed over the hole and two sheets of metal covered each end. There are still today countless of shelters remaining in backyards throughout Britain, a reminder 70 years later, to another generation of what those terrible times were like. I have often wondered what long lost treasures may remain untouched within those silent "humps", that are overgrown or a part of a back garden. These became the nightly home for many people in the city, home at least until dawn, when the final all clear would be sounded with its piercing, but welcome, shrill tone signalling the end of another night of death and destruction. My mother's family would, like their neighbours, emerge bleary-eyed, tired, nervous, fearful, but relieved to see another dawn.

The East End, where my mother and her family grew up and where my grandfather worked in a local meat market and later, after the raids intensified, at the London docks, would be wrought with devastation during the coming months. The area seemed almost to have been singled out for destruction.

West Ham, Stepney, Wapping, Canning Town, the West End, the India area and many other boroughs happened to be near what the Germans saw as key targets. The dockland area, which served shipping from around the world (more than any other port in Britain) was in the same area as armament plants, the world famous Tate & Lyle sugar plant and countless warehouses, in other words, the working heart of London.

Hitler had hoped that by mass bombings and the killing of civilians, the poor of London would cause uprisings and possibly force the English government to sue for peace. If not, at least the bombings would cause enough confusion and destruction to help him in his planned invasion of Britain, 'Operation Sea Lion.' The people of Britain, however, including those of the East End, were not like the people of other countries the Nazis had bombed and now lay under the iron boot of Hitler's Armed Forces. Their response to Hitler was "Britain can take it" and they proved it!

Men like my grandfather, Patrick, many of whom were veterans of the First World War, were tougher than Hitler and his mighty Luftwaffe imagined. They went to work every day, did their jobs, helped fight thousands of the fires that seemed never to end and carried on in the indomitable spirit of the British people. With most of our young Englishmen being called up or already in active service, it was left to people like my grandfather to carry on and take care of his young family. My grandfather fought in the Battle of the Somme and at Mons. While he compared the bombing of London to the shelling he experienced during the First World War, he carried on.

While the city burned, their houses were destroyed and their families killed, terrified children, frightened mothers and grim, determined working-men, continued to show their defiance.

Adolf Hitler with all the military might at his disposal, including the world's most powerful air force (The Luftwaffe) thought he had planned for every eventuality. However, he had not taken into consideration, the will and determination of the people of Great Britain and the people of London and other major cities. Union Jacks sprang up among the bombed-out buildings, signs read, 'Open for business' or 'Business as usual', in buildings that had no shop-fronts. The reality of the nightly attacks and even the death and destruction became a part of life.

As the bombings wore on, all over the East End, homes were gutted and destroyed by the bombings. The smell of acrid gas from ruptured gas lines hung heavy in the air. People began to gather their belongings and those who could, fled the city.

But, the vast majority of these people, who were the backbone of London's working class, stayed behind. Most of them had nowhere to go and in many cases, their children remained with them. These people began to seek safety anywhere. The mothers took their children to air raid shelters. My mother and her family spent many nights in the famous London Underground.

Unfortunately, even though the government had planned for such an event, the Underground could not hold everyone. During normal times, the Underground was where workers would board trains to get to their jobs or head to a store to go shopping. Now it became a source of refuge and safety from the hell being created by the bombing in the city. Terrible and destructive as it was on the streets, below ground a new way of life began. Families gathered, workers in expensive suits from the West End and Mayfair, stood shoulder to shoulder with the men in worn work clothes until the all clear sounded.

When we were at home, and as the Blitz carried on, all the schools were closed, so really we did nothing. My dad went to work and my mother looked for food. The sirens would go off every night about 6.00pm and the unbelievable nightmare would begin all over again. Whenever the bombing started, my brother, Charles, who was truly affected by all this, would sit under the table and scream. My mother and father would take us to the shelter and sit on either side of the shelter with torches. We would come out the next morning only to find ceilings down, windows blown out, no water, gas or electricity. We would have to wait for the Army to bring in water trucks to the streets, which were littered with shrapnel and debris from the raids. During this time, the delayed-action bombs would be exploding everywhere and the fires continued to burn. It was like Hades.

My mother recalled one terrible night of bombing, when her street experienced something no-one had ever been witness to:

My mother had finished feeding the four of us and the boys were playing on the floor in the lounge. Charles had become rather withdrawn. The bombings terrified him and he cried incessantly whenever the sirens began. Dennis, on the other hand, remained silent and only asked my mother what we were to do if the Germans came. This particular night, Marie and I were helping my mother clear up the dinner plates and I had just looked in on the twins who seemed fine. As usual we tried to conduct ourselves as most children our age did, play with our toys and as daughters, Marie and I, were always expected to help our mother in the kitchen. I asked my mum if she thought the Germans might be over tonight. She said what she did every night, "Hopefully not tonight Eileen, they may be after the coastal docks and give London a miss." It was not to be.

At about 9.30pm the sirens began their familiar wail. My mum quickly gathered up the box of necessities we kept in the house and listened for the sirens as they grew louder and closer. She calmly said, "Come on children, let's go out to the shelter and quickly now." Charles had by then crawled under the table and begun to cry. It wasn't the cry you would normally expect out of a child, it sounded more like a whimper, he was so frightened. I knelt down beside him as he huddled under the dining room table and said, "Come on then, out we go, to the back garden and you can play with your truck." As Dennis, Marie, Charles and I started out of the door to the backyard, we could already hear explosions in the distance. As frightened as I was, I tried to be like my mum. "Come on", I said, "Or we will get a piece of mum's mind if we don't hurry."

As we sat huddled in the dark, cold shelter, the raid followed a familiar pattern. You would hear the planes, then the bombs would start to explode, the noises would grow louder and closer, and then the ground would start to shake, and you knew your neighbourhood was in the middle of another night of terror. After all these years, I can still remember clearly how frightened one became when the ground shook. It was the sense of helplessness that was so terrible, sitting in a dirt hole, usually water dripping down the sides of the wooden boards, dirt and debris falling on the top of what was really no more than a hole in your garden. And you waited. I looked at my mother and she smiled and mouthed the words, "It will be all right." She held Marie and Charles close to her and I sat holding Dennis' hand. But that night, unlike most nights, the raid seemed unusually short. The bombing seemed to move away from the East End and the noise of the explosions faded away. While we sat in darkness and waited, we began to hear voices from people in our street. There were shouts of people calling out the names of our neighbours, then suddenly it became quiet, no bombs, no explosions, not even the all too familiar sounds of a fire-engine, or the terrible sound of the ambulances and their distinctive bells ringing, as they raced down the streets looking for victims of the recent attacks.

Shortly after, the 'All Clear' sounded and my mother said the four of us could leave the Shelter. My father was working at the docks that night and, as usual, was not able to come home when the raids started at about 9.00pm.

As the Blitz progressed, the English knew the Germans were literally throwing everything they had at the stubborn residents of London and the people of Great Britain. The variety of bombs that rained down on London was in the words of one historian 'like having the kitchen sink of bombs land on you.' From the small screaming bombs dropped by Stukas, to the 500lb. high explosive bombs that fell from the dreaded Heinkels, to the small but deadly incendiary fire starters that fell from the cigar shaped Doriners. These caused concern, unlike others that were dropped by the Nazis, for their job was to start fires that were difficult to put out. On one memorable raid on London it was these small "fire bombs" that crept within yards of one of the old city's most famous landmarks, St. Paul's Cathedral. Had it not been for the bravery of the fire wardens, the vicars of the church itself, and of the soldiers assigned to assist with the nightly fires, St. Paul's may have been reduced to ashes. Those men on that night truly reflected the indomitable spirit of the British people.

As we emerged from the Anderson shelter, people were out on Libra Road staring at the end of our street. My mum and the boys, Marie and I walked out into the street and saw hanging in a large tree, a giant white parachute. We had seen parachutes before, but this one had a deadly cargo hanging from it, swaying gently in the cold night air...a mine!

The Germans had dropped mines to sink ships. They were attached to parachutes, to gently float down and explode on impact. This was somehow even more terrifying to all of us who stared at it, because the adults knew that it could break loose at any time and would in all likelihood destroy our entire street. People truly began to panic. Mothers started screaming, rushing to gather their children and to run in the opposite direction. People began to fall down in the rush to get away from the bomb. Children were screaming, men were yelling, and I was desperately trying to help my mum gather my brothers and sister and rush to safety.

The problem I remember was utter confusion. As a rush of air seemed to gather momentum from one end of Libra road to the other, the parachute slid down slightly and a few branches began to give way. It was the first time, in those early days of the war I truly felt I would die. But, it always seemed, that even during the most terrifying moments of the Blitz, someone would appear out of the smoke and shadows, even as debris was still falling from the houses, and restore order.

This night was no different; a small army truck sped down the street and out jumped two UXB soldiers (members of the British army's bomb disposal teams). These two unknown heroes, I say unknown because no-one seemed to get their names, calmly walked towards the giant sea mine, while reassuring the terrified residents to move back and get behind whatever shelter we could find. They could not have been much older than 20 or 22 years old and yet they calmly walked to the bomb, climbed the tree and went to work. They began disarming the monster bomb as it gently swung in the cool night air. I never imagined any object could truly look so sinister. But as I look back some seventy years, I remember it like it was yesterday and just the thought of it still sends a chill down my spine. We were fortunate that night that the men from the UXB team did their work with such recently acquired skill and bravery. Many people like me who survived so many terrible nights, owe their lives to those nameless, heroic young men. I know I will never forget them, whoever they were.

After such a night, my grandmother swept away the debris and broken glass from the inside of the house, picked up tree branches that lay in their yard and then went to the kitchen to prepare my grandfather's lunch. He went to work and joined others at their daily jobs and then waited to see if the Germans returned and if they were to face another night of a family's battle to survive.

London was by no means the sole recipient of Hitler's wrath. Manchester, Liverpool, Coventry, Southampton and other cities were visited by the German Luftwaffe and also suffered great damage with a high death toll, cities where my mother's Aunts, Uncles, and other relatives lived and sometimes died. Hull, on the east coast of Yorkshire, was so badly damaged that barely a house was left standing and the Government banned radio and newspapers from broadcasting the news, in case it undermined morale in the rest of Great Britain

But to my mother's family and friends, their war was within the heart of London and in a village called Hatch Beauchamp. During the Blitz it was a personal war. London was ringed with anti-aircraft batteries which were supposed to help defend the city from the bombers, but few bombers were actually ever shot down by this method.

The Ack-Ack guns actual range rarely reached the heights at which the bombers flew, but in a strange way it was comforting for Londoners to know they were giving something back to the Nazis. My mother used to say her mother talked to the other housewives on the street and decided that the anti-aircraft batteries must have downed countless planes in the previous night's raid. There was a comforting, though unnerving sound of an anti-aircraft gun versus the drone of the bombers.

To this day, my mother believes the Heinkel bombers engines sounded as though they were saying 'For you, for you, for you.' Strangely though, history has in a way proved my mother to be correct. Reich Marshall Goering had his pilots and mechanics deliberately set engines out of synch to create a mournful, disconcerting drone of the plane's engines. The purpose was to unnerve the citizens of London and, according to many who lived through that time, Goering's plan worked.

As September painfully passed into night after night of relentless, indiscriminate, destruction of the civilians of London, my mother and her brothers, Dennis and Charles, and her sister Marie did their best to make life on Libra Road normal. Normal, if normal is being bombed from your home, seeing schoolmates die, and watching your mother 'manage coupons', so you can have the basic necessities to eat and wondering every night when your father left for work, if he would return in the morning. Strangely, as their lives settled into a type of routine, after a while, they got used to it.

Another terrible night when it seemed the end had come. We were all in the Anderson shelter and it was sealed shut, as usual, from 6.00pm until 8.00am the next day. An aerial torpedo flew right past the opening, blowing the doors off, and exploding in the next street. It was terrible, my Dad got out and found the doors and sealed us back in the shelter again. I heard him say to my poor mum, "This is worse than anything in Flanders in the last war."

The main reason for my mother's return to Hatch was, by the start of 1941, the people of England were weary of constant nightly raids by the Germans. Things were difficult. The war was not going well. While the threat of invasion had subsided with Hitler's invasion of Russia in June of 1941, a large part of the city of London and various parts of England lay in ruins. Londoners felt they had been singled out for destruction (which to some extent was true). They had taken the best the mighty Luftwaffe could dish out and survived, but there were shortages of most necessities, particularly food, which was now severely rationed and the population was really suffering.

In my mother's house, like many others in the devastated East End, meat, if available, was a luxury once a week. Sweets, oranges, fresh fruit of any kind and the nation's staple, tea, were now in severe shortage. My grandfather took the shortages in his stride, remembering the hardships he had faced as a soldier and dock worker in the First World War, but to the children, it was hard to understand and accept. My grandmother went out every day and stood in queues for hours, it didn't matter what was being sold she joined the line hoping to get some food, any food for her family. The shortages meant anything was worth waiting for if it helped take care of her family. Sadly, by the time she reached the front of the line, in whatever kind of shop, it had frequently sold out, but, like all mothers everywhere, her children had to be fed to survive.

The bombings continued over Britain throughout the spring and into the early summer. Admittedly, the Luftwaffe offensive had lost some of its intensity and the RAF, with the new invention of Radar, began to strike back effectively against the raiders.

However, Londoners still looked nervously to the skies every day and dreaded what the nights would bring. Then on May 10th, the terror returned to London with a vengeance. My mother recalled that night, because six weeks after the May 10th raid, she and her brothers and sister returned to the relative safety of the West Country and Hatch Court. Her family were at home sleeping, as my grandfather had a rare night off from his work on the docks. Shortly after 10.30pm, however, the sirens began to sound their piercing, warning blasts throughout the city, on what was to be one of the last major mass bombing attacks on the city, but it also turned out to be one of the most terrible.

On Saturday May 10, over 541 sorties were flown by the Luftwaffe from 11.30 Saturday night until about 5.30 Sunday morning. German raiders killed more than 1,400 civilians, destroyed over 5,000 houses and left thousands homeless. Some of the victims, like my mother's family, had experienced this before and were once again left homeless. Even with the anti-aircraft fire keeping the bombers higher than they liked, the Germans nonetheless were able to inflict significant damage throughout the city. 2,200 fires raged and over 700 acres of the city were ablaze. Incredibly, the glow of the fires could be seen for the next three days. This was the raid that damaged the Houses of Parliament, Westminster Abbey, Westminster School, Big Ben, Scotland Yard, the Salvation Army headquarters, railway stations, and five of London's hospitals. For the small price of 14 planes, the Luftwaffe had almost created a modern day fire of London, like the one which burnt the city to the ground in 1666.

It has become clear, in researching this book, the stories of the children of London and their parent's recollections of those terrible days and nights, cover the entire spectrum of emotions and experiences. A few years ago the BBC created a forum of the people's war allowing those who lived through the raids of London and surrounding areas to tell their stories. It is an excellent recounting of those dark days, when England and her people stood alone. There is a similar vein that runs through each story, the experience was unique for each one, frightening, exhilarating and it changed forever those who experienced it.

It would be wrong to say that what happened in England was as widespread and destructive as the bombing of cities in Central Europe, Poland, and, of course, Russia, because along with those bombings, came the war on the ground and unspeakable horrors, which by the grace of God (or some say Sir Winston Churchill) was not experienced by Britain because Britain was not invaded. It is therefore not the purpose here to equate the two.

Seventy years after the war, some recent authors believe it is the job of today's generation to soften the horrors of WWII and that the guilt lies only with ardent Nazis, not those who lived in Germany or simply fought in the war on the side of the Germans. It is important to keep in mind that Hitler's intent was to invade England and most likely bring to the British people the same style of 'Liberation' which cost 25 million lives from 1939-1945. History has long since recorded that Germany's desire was to win the war and rule as much territory as she could bring under her influence. Nazis or not, the Germans were out to win.

The will of one man and one people kept Britain from that fate, Winston Churchill and the people who lived, worked, and died in Great Britain. Ask my mother or thousands of people who lived through the Blitz, evacuation, saw death up close and were torn from their lives and loved ones and they will tell you the same thing, over and over again, that it was Sir Winston Churchill who was their inspiration, as much as their innate desire to survive.

Whatever their parents' politics were, their survival depended on a single belief; the faith in Churchill's firm conviction that Britain would not lose, make peace, or allow the Nazis to set foot on their shores. Of course, there were some in Britain who wanted peace at any price, a settlement where Hitler would rule Europe and Britain would operate as a Nazi satellite under German control. Fortunately, the appeasers were not given that chance. Churchill knew 'the people' were his 'ace in the hole and that the workers and ordinary people who had made the 'Empire on which the sun never sets' were not going to bend to 'an Austrian house-painter,' as Churchill once referred to 'Herr Hitler'.

My brothers were becoming more and more hysterical every time the sirens went off, so the decision was made by my parents that we should go back to Hatch Beauchamp. I hated leaving my mother and father again, but my father made us go because of my younger siblings. We went to the bus station the next day and said our tearful goodbyes.

St Paul's Cathedral stands proud during the Blitz

Chapter 7

After the Blitz, the return to the West Country

We arrived back at Hatch Court on a Saturday afternoon in late October 1940, only to find that Mrs Gault had gone up to London to find all the evacuees. Once we arrived we were warmly greeted by everyone, including the 600 members of the Royal Ulster Rifles Regiment, who were camped in the grounds of Hatch Court. They had just come back from Dunkirk and were on manoeuvres on Salisbury Plain, but were actually stationed at Hatch. Whilst we'd been in London, the English Government had begun to evacuate women with babies, so during that short time, Grace Cutteram, Reggie, her mother, two aunts Rose and Lil and their young children had all arrived. The English soldiers were wonderful to us children. They gave us some of their extra 'goodies'...cakes, biscuits and suchlike. They brought their record player and records over to the mess hall and one gentleman in particular, George Mortimer, taught me to dance. He was so kind to all of us. They took pity on us children, because like them we were sort of the 'flotsom' of war. We had a wonderful concert in the Village Hall and I sang and tapped danced for the troops. They loved it and as we walked to school they would stand outside their tents waiting for inspection and shout, "Hey Blondie, give us a tune!" They were there for three weeks and we had a lovely time with sing-songs in the mess-hall. It was really exciting and we were all sorry to see them leave.

In October 1940, I turned 14 and in England in those days everyone left school and went to work. So what was I going to do? Mrs Gault called me up to her bedroom and said there was a position at one of the big houses in another village and she thought it would be suitable for me. I said, "NO, I cannot leave my family." I hoped I would be able to stay and work as a Parlour-maid at the Court, because by this time, most of the servants had been called up; Mills the Butler had gone, Frank the Footman had gone, the Cook had gone, Betty Yard, the upstairs maid had gone.

Just before I left that fall (Autumn), my mother came down, and the four of us moved into a farm cottage, but we were not there very long. My dad, who worked at the London Docks, often could not get home at nights because of the air raids and my mother felt she should be with him in London, so she went back to London and we went back to Hatch Court.

I then put on my uniform and began to work as a parlour-maid for one pound, one shilling & sixpence a month. Mrs Gault really changed at this time. She called me up to her bedroom and said, "From now on, you must call me 'Madam' and must stand up when I come into the room". As I walked out of the room I felt as though I was something that had lost everything and was a non-person. Ever since I had been sent to Hatch, I could see what was considered the 'British Class System'. The war changed that. There were only the four of us siblings left there, as well as some of the evacuee women who were still there with their babies, so we lived in a world that lacked a sense of belonging.

Marie, Dennis and Charles lived under the Clock Tower and I moved to the 'Top Landing' with the rest of the servants; Joan, the housemaid, Rogers, the head housemaid, Evelyn, the scullery maid and Betty, the cook. Frank, the footman had been called up, so had Mills, the butler and Alice, the 'second' housemaid. Life went on and I was taught how to set the dining room table; how to place cutlery, glasses, clean silver, carry a tray and wait on the table. I enjoyed it when the Brigadier & Mrs Gault had dinner parties, mostly military officers from all branches of the services. They included British, lots of Canadians, South Africans and Polish Airmen, all in their assortment of uniforms and all the ladies in beautiful evening gowns. On these occasions, Joan and I would serve them, but I also played tricks and did terribly childish things to make Joan laugh. She would have to run out and stand in the hall laughing so no-one could see her.

We were given one day off a week and every other Sunday. I spent my free time doing several things. I would go on the 1.30pm bus into Taunton to see the movies. (We called them 'the pictures' in those days) I loved the movies, they were our only escape. I watched every musical that was ever made during the war and saw Betty Grable, Rita Hayworth, Esther Williams and all the Big Bands. I just loved them all. Nothing could be bought without coupons, but if I saw a *queue, whatever was for sale, I'd line up and get whatever they were selling; a comb, toothpaste or anything like that.*

Dances were also held around the villages and I would always 'ask/beg' Mrs Gault to let me go. I would borrow someone's bike, put my silver shoes in a bag, pin my dress around my neck, put on my slacks and off I'd go to the dances!

After one of my evening outings, I walked up the drive to Hatch to a terrible commotion with fire engines and the police. The hayricks were on fire. As I got closer, every farmer in the village was there and the first person I met was Mrs Gault's mother, Mrs. Shuckburgh.

I asked, "Who started the fire?" She said, "The twins." I was horrified. She was busying herself looking for her diamond earring that had fallen off. I then saw Dennis and Charles who were with a boy they had been playing with, who apparently had made a small fire in a tin can and kicked it amongst the hay. Everyone blamed it on my twin brothers.

The farmers decided that Dennis and Charles should be 'sent away'. Mrs Gault called me into her bedroom and said it had been decided to 'send them away'. (Could anyone really have thought I would let my brothers be taken away?) I told her, if they go, then Marie and I must go with them. We could not be separated, as my father had said so before we left London. Her response was 'Rubbish, we can't allow that'. We ended up staying at Hatch throughout the war, even though years later the villagers still thought Dennis and Charles had started that fire! They didn't set that fire, Mrs Gault was correct; it was 'rubbish'.

Eileen was very protective of her family. Nothing negative could ever be said about her brothers and sister without her immediately coming to their defence. I suppose it was always that way and my mother felt they were blamed for things because they were evacuees from London and not village children. She has never forgotten that being from the East End did not endear her to some of the local people of Hatch Beauchamp and one of the events that was blamed on her brothers, which she was sure was not their fault, was the haystack fire of 1940. She has always contended that another evacuee named Frank set the fire and her twin brothers were accused of doing it because they were easy 'marks' (easy to blame). In fact, as she related this event she concluded that the local farmers, Mrs Gault, and even the other evacuee boys were all wrong. She dismissed the very suggestion of sending her brothers away from Hatch just because the local farmers were upset over the fire, as something she simply could not allow.

She was as much a parent to my uncles as a sister. In some ways, more so, because with her lack of experience, she simply acted on instinct and did not entertain the fact that her family might be separated. After all, she had promised her father that his children would stay together. The war made every one grow up fast and my mother's family were no exception and even now, nearly seventy years later, she has always maintained her brothers were unjustly accused of the fire incident.

It was not until April 2010, when I visited Hatch Beauchamp as a guest of John Townsend and was able to speak to a few remaining locals who remembered the war, that the truth of what happened the night of the fire was brought to light.

In speaking to the locals, they told me they all remembered my mother and her family and in the same breath would say, 'Oh, yes and we remember the twins starting the fire in the hay stack.' After listening to their stories, I returned to my Aunt's house in Ilford, somewhat confused. You see, my mother had always said that everyone was wrong; her brothers never started any fire. As I sat in the lounge talking to my two aunts (my uncles' widows) about the tales I had heard in Hatch Beauchamp about their husbands and the story of the fire, I asked them if their husbands had ever mentioned it to them? They both said that they had heard the story and that Dennis and Charles had told them that they had started the fire. So, apparently my mother has been wrong for 70 odd years. Her brothers did, indeed, start the fire, agreed to blame it on another boy and stuck to that story for many years. Somehow, although I was not involved in this controversy, I felt like I had solved the mystery of the lost city of Atlantis.

Throughout my 57 years, I have rarely known my mother make major mistakes, but on this occasion, as a result of her love for her brothers and her desire to defend and protect them, she obviously made a big one.

Various regiments stayed at Hatch Court, including the Grenadier Guards and a tank regiment. After Dunkirk, deep trenches were dug across the whole of England. A trench was dug at Hatch Court which stretched across the bottom of the drive, by men from various countries who escaped with the B.E.F. (British Expeditionary Force).

They still had bandages covering their wounds as they dug the trenches. We would pass them on our way to school and they would always give us the 'V' for Victory sign as they could not speak any English.

This trench was part of a series of many defence lines the British prepared across various parts of the country, in case of a German invasion. According to Hitler's plans, Operation Sea Lion was scheduled for September 1940. Once the Royal Air Force had been subdued, it was generally believed the Nazis would launch an invasion of the British Isles. Part of the plan of the British government to stop or disrupt such an invasion was to build a series of fortified positions that would criss-cross the island and turn various villages and towns into strong defensive positions.

In the area around Taunton, which included Hatch Beauchamp, this became known as the Taunton Deane Stop Line. Running from roughly Clevedon in the north to Chard in the south, through the West Country, this was to be where the war would be fought when the Nazis arrived. In the Taunton area alone, there were over 355 pillboxes, countless anti-tank obstacles, well over 112 forts and 233 various airfield defences. Scattered throughout the countryside in key points were outposts of the Observer Corps. These small, self contained locations were to identify aircraft which approached their locations, report paratrooper landings and, ultimately to call out the Home Guard to actually assist the Army in fighting the invaders. The Home Guard were known as the Local Defence Volunteers (LDV) at the start of the war, but in spite of the fact that many of their members ranged from farmers to highly decorated veterans of the First World War, they were in many circles considered more of a potential liability than an asset to the Army. They spent many hours practising, sometimes with only pikes and pitchforks, in case, at a moment's notice, Britain needed them to help defend their country against the most highly trained army in the world, the German Wermacht.

What my mother witnessed around Hatch, alongside Dunkirk veterans digging the anti-tank trench and building various village fortifications, were men from countries which had already been overrun by the Nazis. They had survived the Dunkirk evacuation, and even though defeated on the field of battle, were not defeated in spirit. They were willing (almost without exception) to give their last full measure of devotion to a country many of them had never seen before early June 1940.

I remember, for many weeks, seeing these brave men at work day after day. At night we could look out to the fields surrounding Hatch Court and see tiny streaks of light and hear muffled voices as these men worked around the clock, all over the fields, in some cases, digging with little more than trench shovels (short, folding shovels issued to soldiers in their personal kit of equipment when they went into combat) *to complete their work. I often think of how these men, when they had finished, moved* on to the next village and repeated the same tasks. I asked the Brigadier, on more than one occasion, as did the other children, "What can we do to help these men?" He would look at all of us and say, "If you have something extra, share it with them. Say hello to them, stop and give them water if you can." I could not grasp at the time why these men had officers walking amongst them barking orders to pick up the pace here, dig wider or deeper there, quick step now down the country lane to repeat the process all over again. To us they had done enough and were in many cases wounded and deserved a rest. But, there was no rest for these men, or thousands of others working on our defences. Little did I know that there was really only a faint hope that these men, their trenches, the forts, and members of the Home Guard could ever be expected to stop the invading army which was expected any day.

One day Mrs Gault and Mrs Shuckburgh made a trip to Ilminster, about 5 miles away, which I think had something to do with Mrs Gault's Red Cross duties. I can now not even recall why Marie and I went with them, but, as we drove towards Ilminster, which I had been to a few times since our arrival in September of 1939, I realized the countryside had dramatically changed. Ilminster had become a fortress. All around the beautiful countryside there were antitank ditches, barbed wire, concrete forts and pillboxes and close to Dillington House, there was a newly constructed large fortress-type building. We had been told the Germans were planning to invade and seeing these things close to, made me think that we were going to be evacuated again, from our new home at Hatch Court, to another part of the country. Thankfully it never came to that.

On my first visit to Hatch Beauchamp in 1985, my Aunt Janet drove me around the area, looking at fields and towns, to see if there were any remnants of the war years left. I was surprised at how much could still be seen, even to a casual observer like me. I was in disbelief in what remained, forty years after the end of the war.

There were runways of abandoned air bases in fields where cows now grazed. I saw pillboxes in farmers' fields that stood as silent sentinels that were ready to repel an invasion that never came; anti–tank blocks (known later in the war as Dragon's teeth) by a river canal near Curry Mallet; they were to stop the tanks of the invading German Armoured Divisions that were never used.

Everywhere we went, I saw in the shadows of trees and the overgrown parts of farmland, remnants of the determination of the British people, who in desperation and with undaunted courage, had built defences to repel an invader, who by the grace of God, never came. Twenty five years later as I drove again through the small villages and fields, it was pointed out to me, by John Townson, that some of those defensive preparations still remained intact. We stopped the car and he pointed out an overgrown trench, a pillbox in the corner of a field and an observation post with an underground escape hatch that fortunately was never used. For someone who takes pride in his English roots, it occurred to me for the first time in my life, that with little more than bluff and bluster in the darkest days of the Second World War, the people of Great Britain had indeed been prepared to die for their country, way of life and their freedom from oppression.

Charles and Dennis aged 6

Servants' Entrance – Hatch Beauchamp

Chapter 8

Everyday life as an evacuee
1939 – 1945

During the years as an evacuee at Hatch, life was always filled with mixed emotions. There were sad times, happy times and times when I felt nothing. Being an evacuee was a new life, a different life, a life of uncertainty. So as the initial fear and excitement started to subside, I settled into a new, but fairly regular routine.

We went to school every day, of course, but before we could go to school, we would have to get a basket and go over to Hescombe's and pick mushrooms for breakfast for the 'front' of house. We always came back with baskets full. Then during school, we used to have to pick gunny sacks full of stinging nettles and give them to the WVS (Women's Voluntary Service). They were used for the quinine, which was sent to the troops in the Far East, to help combat Malaria.

On Sundays, we went to the beautiful little church of St John the Baptist, which was located just behind the Court. The Brigadier and Mrs Gault loved it when they walked up through the garden with all 11 of us children and we would all pile into the 'reserved' pews inside the church. We listened to the sermons and sang hymns. Once, when we were all in church, I sat next to the Brigadier. My mother would send us sixpence a week spending money. When Joan's uncle, who was a church warden, brought the collection plate round, I couldn't bear to put my whole sixpence on the plate, so I said, "Could you give me change?" The Warden just looked at me with displeasure. The Brigadier put a shilling on the plate and said, 'This is for Eileen.' The Brigadier was such a lovely man.

For fun, lots of times in the evenings we would have what we called a 'pick'. Our names were put into a hat and someone would pick out a name and whoever's name was chosen could go to see something wonderful in the front of the house. You see, we were never allowed in the front of the house except on special occasions. That 'something wonderful' might be the lion's skin (a real lion's skin), the Brigadier's sword, the mounted buffalo head or the mounted moose head. We all stood by the loggia and waited until the lucky person came back and told us the wonders they had seen.

During these events, Mrs Gault's nieces were sometimes staying there. We were instructed to call them Miss Ann, Miss Hazel and Miss Veronica. It made us all feel rather inferior and with a lack of self-esteem. But, there was more class separation in those days and we, being from the East End, were of a different class. After Mrs Gault gave Betty and Evelyn 2 days a week off, she thought that Ann Sykes (her niece) and her friend could learn to cook. I am not sure how the cooking lessons turned out, all I know is that the four of us; Grace, Rose, Marie and I would come home from school and spend almost 2 hours washing the dishes, pots and pans, until our hands were raw, but as they were members of the family and I was a servant and evacuee, I was not given thanks for my efforts. However, Ann and Hazel were always warm with their treatment of Marie, the boys and me.

By October of 1940 I had become a parlour maid. So for five years, upon waking I started my day by cleaning the fireplace grate and polishing all the black fire-irons (which were tools used to stoke fires). Then I would scrub the floors, clean the brass and then move to upstairs. Upstairs consisted of the maids' quarters which I would clean, their rooms and bath areas. At lunchtime, I would change my uniform and serve lunch in the dining room, wash the dishes and prepare the afternoon tea for Mrs Gault and guests. This was just another routine to get used to.

However, being away from London did not mean the war was not close by. On many nights, we heard bombing in the distance and sometimes the bombs were close by. In early November of 1940, when we had been back from London for only a few weeks, the Germans began to bomb and attack nearby towns and villages. I returned from Taunton on the 4th of November, after going to town with Mrs Gault and some of the children, to buy food and Mrs Gault had also been to a meeting of the Red Cross. On the very next day, it was reported that a low flying German plane had machine-gunned the streets in Taunton. Whenever there was a condition RED or an alert, Mrs Gault would put on her Red Cross uniform and help wherever she was needed. Shortly after that, bombs were dropped at the Naval Air Station at Yeovil. It seemed to us that bombing might even occur at Hatch Beauchamp.

Although about 5 miles from Taunton, Hatch appeared to be in the flight path of German planes. Nearby Wrantage had been bombed terribly. This was the night that Eve, Betty, Alice and I decided to sleep out on the roof. We had all kind of goodies to eat and we laughed and giggled all night until about 2.30am, when we heard a terrible noise, which sounded to be very close by. A Junker 88 flew past and dropped a bomb in Wrantage. Needless to say, we climbed back into my room, collapsed on the floor with hysterical laughter, but we were really scared to death. I was petrified that Mrs Gault could hear us, as my bedroom was above hers. If she was not calling me, 'up the carpet', she was pounding on her ceiling every morning, to make sure I was up. I just knew for sure she would pound on her ceiling any moment.

Taunton continued to be the victim of German raids, and Weston-Super-Mare was repeatedly attacked with much destruction and many deaths. The other children and I were reassured by Brigadier Gault that Hatch had no real military importance and it was highly unlikely that the Germans would drop a bomb on our small village. However, nearby Staple FitzPaine and West Hatch had been victims of German bombing in April that year and I could not get over a growing fear that we too would be victims. What really worried me as a young girl was that my brothers and sister remained frightened after returning from London after the Blitz. Some had not been so lucky for they became victims of the Blitz. My younger brother Charles developed a slight stutter as a result of what he had been through and it stayed with him for the rest of his life.

Looking back on it now, it must have been dreadful for Dennis and Charles, but more especially Marie. That young girl carried a heavy burden, taking care of the boys, cooking, cleaning and sitting in that mess hall night after night. She always hugged the boys, but there was no one there to give her a hug. I used to see the three of them walking through the passage at lunch time. Marie would pick up their plates from the kitchen and they would sit in that old stone floored mess-room and eat their lunch. She would then wash up their plates and go back to school. I feel that I didn't do enough for her or for the boys for that matter. One day, as I was in the bathroom, I happened to look out of the window and saw Dennis running down the drive with something in his hand. I ran after him and he was almost at the 'Silver Gate' when I caught him. He had saved his sixpence and he said, "I am going back home to London, I am running away." I told him, "Dennis, you cannot, you have to stay here." I just held him as we both lay down on the grass and cried. I thought, "Poor kid, poor Dennis, poor Charles and Marie."

It wasn't until the boys turned 10 that they started going to school in Ilminster. They rode on the bus every day and if they missed it, they had to walk the six miles to school. One day when they missed the bus and were walking to school they found a bazooka at the side of the road. They told the police. Thank God they didn't touch it! The police drove them on to school. The boys found great excitement in that and talked about it a lot. This was about the same time that the boys were finally allowed to go into the front hall with the Brigadier and Mrs Gault. After the Gaults finished their dinner, they all sat in the front hall, around the fire, and talked. The Brigadier told them stories and the boys just loved it. It was a real treat for them.

There were times when Mrs Gault received a 'red' air raid warning. She told us to get out of bed and we all went down into the cellar. Dear Evelyn told us stories about Brer Fox and Brer Rabbit to keep us entertained. Evelyn was one of the good people I will never forget. Sometimes, on Sundays, she felt sorry for us and took one of us home with her to West Hatch to her family. It was wonderful to be in a house and have a lovely fire and tea. Her brother, Bunny, was sometimes home on leave. He was with the Somerset Light Infantry. He too always made us laugh. It felt good to laugh, for in those days, there didn't seem much to laugh about.

During the winter of 1940-1941 it was very cold, but it was nothing compared to the winters to come in the next 4 years. Although my parents had sent us winter coats, we always felt cold. One early evening as the sky darkened, probably in February or March of 1941, I was walking home from the village, down Curry Mallet Road which ran in front of Hatch Court and into Hatch Beauchamp. I was walking fast and had my head down to try to keep warm. I was by myself, as the boys were already at the house and Marie was with the other children at the Clock Tower. Mrs Gault always said 'Walk fast and keep an eye to the sky.' We had seen German planes and from time to time actual dogfights as the brave pilots of the RAF fought day after day with the German fighters and bombers, but when a battle takes place 20,000 feet above you, it is impossible to tell who is winning. As I approached the main drive, the sound of a far-off plane grew louder and louder, until it almost seemed to be right above me. As I looked up, I saw a Dornier bomber making a lazy turn over the fields around Hatch. I knew planes that had bombed Bristol or the famous airfield at Biggin Hill sometimes made their turns in the Somerset area near Taunton as they headed back to France. I had just never seen one so close and flying so low. As I began to run towards the main drive, I heard a noise that sounded like the popping of a continuous stream of fireworks. It seemed as though it lasted for an eternity, but in reality it was only a few seconds. The field beside me and the trees that lined the road made a sound similar to a strong wind rustling through a forest, but it was not the wind, it was bullets tearing at the tree branches and scattering livestock. I was experiencing my first sounds of a plane firing its machine guns. I ran as fast as I could and as I looked over my shoulder, the plane was rising into the darkening sky. He must have decided to get a better look at the area and, if nothing else, frighten the cattle grazing in the field, but at that moment, I thought the plane had seen me and was firing its machine guns at me.

On reflection, I doubt if the pilot even saw me walking down the road, but, for a few days I was convinced that plane had been trying to shoot at me. I arrived back at Hatch and told Marie what had happened. She asked me if I was all right and then, in what I considered one of my darling sister's lifetime understatements, she asked, 'Were you frightened?' As I stood breathlessly before her and eventually began to stop shaking, I could only laugh, which was better than crying, and say, "Yes Marie, I was very scared."

As time went on, Betty and Evelyn went to work at the Naafi and Alice and Joan were called up to do War Work.

There was only Rodgers left, as she was too old to go to war. Rosemary Napper came as the kitchen maid. She was a good hearted country girl. Her family lived on the edge of the woods on the Estate. Old Napper was the woodsman and his brother, Reggie, was the trapper. Poor Rosemary had had such a terrible life with her father, so I suppose working at The Court was a great relief for her.

After all the changing of the staff due to the war, there were now only three maids, Rodgers, the upstairs maid, Rosemary and me. There were still two cooks who were there from before the war, Mrs Raddon and Mrs Brown. Mrs Raddon, who was the cook and housekeeper, treated us as though we were slaves. She was a living horror as she tried to run the house as it was before the war with a full staff. She never called us by our names just 'Young Maid'. I told her my name was Eileen which made no difference to her. I got fed up one day and told her "I'm not carrying this tray until you call me by my right name." She took a fit, had a huge knife in her hand, and banged it so hard on the table that the whole top broke off. She called me Eileen after that.

One day, Rosemary and I went into Taunton and when we got back we were starving hungry, so we went into the larder and put some cheese, bread and beets on a plate and sat in the servants' hall and ate it. Mrs Raddon raised hell and told Mrs Gault that we were stealing the food. Mrs Gault called me up to her bedroom 'on the carpet', and asked me what I thought I was doing. I told her I felt like throwing myself under a bus. She went white and told me never to talk that way in this house again. I told her we hadn't had anything to eat since noon. She said we could always have supper when we came back from our day off. Anyway, Mrs Raddon left soon after that.

Mrs Brown, who was absolutely terrible, treated Marie and the boys in a dreadful manner. She served them the rib cage of a rabbit and hardly anything else for supper. It upset me the way they were all alone in that horrible mess-hall. It truly seemed as though no-one cared about them.

Fresh food was increasingly hard to come by as most staples had begun to be rationed as early as late 1939. Along with butter, meat and milk, one of the staples of the English diet was eggs. The rationing of eggs had an effect on the English diet, almost as severe as if tea had been rationed (which was, indeed, a victim of government rationing). At Hatch Court, my mother's family along with the other evacuees, experienced the same shortages as almost everyone in England.

My mother, as the oldest in her family, always felt a responsibility to see that her brothers and sister were fed. When she became a parlour-maid at Hatch, she served wonderful dinners to guests of the Gaults. While she held no animosity towards them about what they ate, there was continuous conflict with the servants who ran the kitchen, as to what the evacuees would eat, which my mother felt was very unfair. Given the archaic attitude of the cook, Mrs Brown, it was simply a matter of time before my mother and her would do battle over the food allotted to the evacuee children.

Some years ago mother, relayed to me the story of the 'Great Egg Caper' and the battle that ensued between her and Mrs Brown. Mother was returning dishes to the kitchen after serving lunch to the Brigadier, Mrs Gault and some guests. Mrs Brown ordered my mother to move quickly with the dessert plates and, in no uncertain terms, told her she thought she was lagging behind in the performance of her duties. Apparently my mother's response was to remind Mrs Brown that she was 'the cook' not the lady of the house and turned quickly into the pantry to retrieve some biscuits. While in the pantry she almost knocked over a large earthenware pot with a lid on it. She grabbed the lid to put it back on properly, but before she did, she looked into the pot. To her surprise, it was full of fresh eggs in isinglass (a preservative for eggs, a kind of syrupy liquid or jelly made from fish bladders, which by the way today is a component used in glue – not the most mouth watering substance). She thought to herself *"My God, they have been hiding fresh eggs!"*

After she retrieved the biscuits, she asked Mrs. Brown if she could get an egg or two for the children. She was told in terms she could not have possibly misunderstood that the eggs were the property of the Gaults and they were not to be eaten by the 'Bloody Evacs' as they were often referred to by Mrs Brown and other locals.

The 'gauntlet had definitely been thrown down' by Mrs Brown to my mother who was determined to relieve Mrs Brown of her precious eggs and give some to the children. So that night, after Mrs. Brown had retired to her room above the kitchen, my mother began her quest. With the stealth that would have made a commando proud, she silently left her room in the upstairs front of the house and made her way through the dark hallways, down the back stairs and into the main kitchen which held the treasure. Her goal – the liberation (not actual theft, mind you!) of the fresh eggs that were nestled in the old earthenware pot. Her purpose was to see to it that the younger children enjoyed a fresh egg.

Mother recalled that all they ever had were powdered eggs, that fresh eggs were a thing of the past. While Hatch Court was part farm, part woodlands, much of what was produced at the farm was sold or, as was common, a certain amount of fresh food, produce and dairy products were requisitioned by the government for the troops. Apart from that, the Gaults as was to be expected, consumed food from the farm. As a result, little was left for the evacuees.

So, once in the pantry, she quietly lifted the lid from the sacred tomb and placed the four eggs into a small bowl, then crept up the backstairs to her room, hid the bowl under her bed and drifted off to sleep. She had beaten Mrs Brown, or so it seemed.

Very early the next morning, even before Mrs Brown was up, mother took the eggs into the kitchen, cooked them, cleaned up the evidence and enjoyed a wonderful breakfast of real eggs with the children. Mission accomplished.

But, as with most clandestine operations, many times seemingly little things are overlooked and those oversights can spell disaster. Such would be the case for my mother. Her brother Charles was so excited to have enjoyed fresh eggs, he couldn't wait to share his good fortune with a fellow evacuee who lived in the house. As with most children, Reggie approached Mrs Brown and asked if he too would be getting an egg.

When my mother came into the kitchen to get the plates and silverware for lunch, Mrs Brown exploded into a tirade about four stolen eggs and the children eating food that was property of the Gaults. Caught red handed, my mother desperately tried to explain they had not had fresh eggs for so long and she had done it only for the children. At that moment it occurred to my mother that no-one but her knew it had actually been her that had pilfered four eggs – until now. She quietly asked Mrs. Brown *"How do you know there are four eggs missing?"* Amazingly Mrs. Brown responded, 'I count them – daily.'

With that being the case, she was duly reported to Mrs Gault who proceeded, while slightly amused, to call my mother to account for taking food which truly was not hers. While once again being 'called upon the carpet' my mother assured Mrs Gault her days of planning midnight kitchen visits were indeed over.

Over half a century later, mother still carries a grudge against the long departed Mrs Brown for 'turning her in'. However, she remembers that the eggs were indeed most delicious, and the effort and scolding were well worth it.

Finally, Mrs Gault said they could all eat in the servants' hall. They came in and sat down and Mrs Brown said, 'You are not to speak while eating.' The poor kids sat there scared to death. I asked Marie, "How was school today?" Marie was even afraid to answer me. I said, "Marie, answer my question." Mrs Brown shouted, 'No talking!' I then picked up a jar of jam and threw it across the table. Everyone went nuts, but from that point on, everyone was allowed to speak.

After that, poor Marie was suffering from malnutrition and was covered in boils. She was very sick and had to stay in bed. It was pitiful to watch my little sister suffer so. The Doctor came and lanced a huge carbuncle she had on her arm. We were strictly on our own and I will never understand why Mrs Gault just turned a deaf ear to some of the things which went on. At times Mrs Gault, as lady of the house, was occupied with her own life and that of the Brigadier. Looking back, I realize that we were evacuees, not guests at Hatch. My three younger siblings seemed to live without love from anyone. I didn't care for myself, but for them I felt so sad.

Yet Marie really loved Mrs Gault. She would pick violets and primroses and put them in Mrs Gault's bedroom. But Rodgers really resented anything Marie did for Mrs Gault, so she was not allowed to do it anymore. Marie was the only girl left and I now realise how lonely she must have been.

By that time Marie had left school, and with nowhere to go, went to work in the kitchen. She used to scrub those flagstones on her hands and knees. What a sorry lot the two of us were.

If you wanted to have fun, you would have to create it. One day, when the Gaults had gone to Scotland and Mrs Shuckburgh to Budliegh Salterton, where she had a small home near the coast, Joan and I were sitting in the pantry when I said to Joan, "Let's go upstairs and try on Mrs Gault's evening gowns." The poor girl almost collapsed. We went upstairs to Mrs Gault's bedroom and I tried on all her evening gowns. There were beautiful long velvet evening gowns in royal blue and green; pale pink and apricot chiffons, some with pearls and beads. They were so very lovely and I felt like a queen wearing them. I had on the royal blue velvet gown and jumped up on Mrs Gault's dressing table stool, started singing and acting the fool. By this time Joan was near hysterics, laughing so hard I thought she was going to pass out. She kept running to the window to make sure no-one was coming back, for she was sure we were going to get caught. I didn't care, I was having so much fun. I neatly put everything back like I found them. No one ever knew of our little fashion show.

One evening, when Rosemary was going up to the farm to get the bucket of milk to bring back to the house, Eve, Dolly and I got some white sheets, ran up to the church yard and stood on the gravestones and waited for the poor girl. It was almost dark and when she came down from the farm bringing the milk, we raised our arms with white sheets flapping and howled like ghosts! Well, the bucket and milk went flying as Rosemary took off like a shot. She almost died with fright. We were laughing so hard almost doubling over. But then I felt so bad afterwards because she was really frightened. What a mean thing for us to do. I guess I should say a mean thing for me to do as it was my idea. But that didn't stop my antics. A few days later, I tied a dead mouse to the door knob in the kitchen. As Rosemary reached for the door knob she grabbed hold of the dead mouse, and once again I thought she was going to have a fit for she screamed out so loudly, which in turn scared me. I really don't know who was more scared her or me? I don't recall ever scaring poor Rosemary again.

An exciting time for me was when I joined the Junior Red Cross along with other girls from the surrounding villages. We used to march in all the parades in Taunton, the War Weapons Week, Spitfire Week, Royal Navy Week and so on. Before we could do this, we had to learn how to march, so the Brigadier had a British Sergeant Major come out from Taunton Barracks to teach us. We wore our uniforms, and all assembled in the courtyard. He marched us around the front of the house where the Brigadier took the salute on the Loggia; he would stand as if he was reviewing his Regiment. We wore navy blue berets and, of course, I wore mine on the side of my head. He took one look and said to Mrs Gault, 'Dorothy, we have a Parisian model with us this evening.' As we marched up to him and gave the 'eyes right', of course, my hat fell off in the dirt. Everyone marched over it. Far be it for me to stop and pick it up. Anyway we marched until we got it right, and by the time I retrieved my cap, it was in a shape that hardly resembled a Parisian model's.

Then, whenever the parade was arranged, which was always on a Saturday, Rosemary and I would ride the bikes to Taunton. We would march about 6 miles then ride back to Hatch. Almost every Saturday night there was a dance in one of the villages, in Curry Mallet, North Curry or Five Head. I would absolutely beg Mrs Gault to go, and it all depended on her mood. If she did say 'yes', I would change into my uniform, hurry to serve dinner, get dressed, pin my dress around my neck, put on my slacks under my dress, sling my silver shoes in the saddle bag and off we'd go. Sometimes we would cycle almost 6 miles to a dance in a barn, but anything to escape. We always had to have a front light and a back light on the bicycles. Sometimes I'd just tie a flashlight on the back, cover it with lipstick so that it would glow red, then off I'd go.

The saddest day for me was in May 1941. As I was on my way up stairs to put up freshly folded towels, I noticed a letter on the entry table addressed to Mrs Gault from Gracie Hill. Gracie Hill was a dear friend of our family who lived in London. She was like a mother to me. I couldn't understand why Gracie would be writing to Mrs Gault.

About 3.00pm that afternoon, Mrs Gault called me upstairs. She informed me that my mum was seriously ill. She had been doing war work for the Royal Navy, making rope. While at work, a landmine had exploded, and everyone had dashed outside to seek safety. While my mum was running out, she tripped over some fallen debris, fell and cut her face. Apparently she didn't think much about it at the time. However, infection set in, and since there was no proper medicine or antibiotics available she became very ill.

The next day, once again Mrs Gault called me up to her room to inform me that my mum had indeed died of cellulitis. I was devastated and so heartbroken that I couldn't even speak. My thoughts were running amuck. My poor mum, my poor father. I quickly realized the task that was before me. I had to tell my sister, now 12, and two brothers of 9, the terrible fate of our mum. What a horrible day for the four of us. Shortly after, my dad sent Marie and me black and white checked dresses and the two boys black armbands. I felt so sorry for all of us. It was hard to realize my mother was gone, no goodbyes, no last visit with her for us, it was indeed an empty feeling.

I went back to London during the autumn for a short holiday and stayed with Aunt Lil Walker. I went to see my Dad, where he still lived on Libra Road. When I saw my poor Father on his hands and knees washing the kitchen floor, I could not believe it. My Dad had never had to move a cup while my mother was alive, and here he was scrubbing the kitchen floor. I wanted to cry. I looked around the house and almost everything was gone that had belonged to my mother; cups, saucers, plates, dishes, everything. When I asked him where they had gone, he said my Aunt Lil had taken everything. He truly did not seem to care at that point. Aunt Lil and Joe had had the keys to the house and were slowly stealing everything and my Dad never even noticed. After the war, when I asked my dad what had happened to my mother's things, I realized it wasn't that he didn't know things were gone, he really just didn't care.

While I was at home there were terrible air raids. It was all so frightening that I went back to Hatch. I really hated my life and there was nothing I could do about it. Then my Dad came down for a week to see us. He seemed to enjoy his visit and old Durman would take him around the old Inns, and we went to the cinema with him, but he remained dressed in black and I knew then he was still lonely, and longing for my mother. By this time, Mrs Gault had moved the boys and Marie to the 'top landing'. They were happier there. I shared a room with Rosemary much of the time, because my room was in one of the 'towers' where there was still a blackout problem.

During the war you sometimes had to find humour in things that you normally would not find amusing, and during those days I met many characters, and there were many people who influenced my later life. One of those people, who I will always remember fondly, was Mrs Gault's mother, Blanche Shuckburgh. She was truly a lady from the 19th century who always showed her wry sense of humour, at times to make light of situations that others in the house took too seriously. She was a beautiful lady who I imagine enjoyed the social whirl of London society in the early days of her life. I got to know her better than the other evacuees who lived at Hatch Court. She had an obsession with keeping the silver clean; I sometimes thought that was part of her war effort. Almost every morning she came into the pantry with gloves on and asked, "Who will help me clean the silver?" I don't think she ever realized none of us wanted to clean silver. It really didn't matter, as we did it whether we liked it or not.

She also gave of her time in Taunton, throughout the war, by going into Taunton and helping to roll bandages for the Red Cross. She was I think, from time to time, less than pleased with the antics of myself and others in the house. We were, of course, no more than children, and she would walk by us, throw her hands up in the air and shake her head at something we were doing. I think she struggled with a house full of children, who entered her life when she had grown older.

I look back on her as someone who tried to cling to the life she had before the war, but that was part of her charm. Time after time, when I was working in the house, she gently reminded of things I needed to do (in a way which I look back on fondly as 'nudges') of things I needed to do. Often I forgot to do what I considered of little importance, such as sweeping crumbs off the dining table and she would say, 'Eileen we mustn't forget the crumbs,' and point out to me barely visible table crumbs left over from bread, or whatever it happened to be. It was, indeed, part of her charm; war was all around her and Mrs Shuckburgh, through it all, was making sure the table remained immaculate.

Each year upon Mrs Shuckburgh's birthday, we went to pick blackberries for her birthday tart. One year I wouldn't go. Someone in the kitchen told Mrs Gault and she called me up to her bedroom. I always referred to this summons as 'Up on the carpet', since I seemed to have worn a path on the carpet from being called up there so often over the years. She told me that refusing to do what I was told was not an option. As you might imagine, I was a participant in future blackberry pickings and Mrs Shuckburgh always had her blackberry tart.

One day she walked into the kitchen and asked me to help her gather flowers from the garden. I said, "I can't, I would have to take my roller skates off". (My sister Marie had been to London to visit my parents and brought back my skates, which were important to a young girl back then). I had been having a wonderful time, in the previous days, skating all through the courtyard and through the kitchen area when no-one was around. I skated to the kitchen table and she looked at me as if I was a mental case, and said, "Skates?" I believe she was not sure I meant roller skates and she gave me a look and walked out of the pantry. As she left, she turned and said to me, "Eileen, you must not wear the skating items in the main house." The servants who were in the room with me, all became hysterical at her reaction, but she never said a word to anyone. I know Mrs Gault would not have been happy with someone roller skating in her home, but I didn't care.

Mrs Shuckburgh was amazed by how young people behaved. Bob phoned the house one day to speak to me. Mrs Shuckburgh stopped me in the main hall and told me my American boyfriend had called, and that when he hung up he had not addressed her as 'Madam'. She told me to tell Bob never to call the house again. This was not said to be mean to me, but to her it was simply not an acceptable way to behave. I couldn't wait to tell him and hear his reaction. When I told him, he said, "Tell that lady that the term 'Madam' has a different meaning in the States, and it is not meant to be flattering". Of course, I told her what Bob had said and without missing a step she shot back, "Well, tell your friend he is in England now, and in England gentlemen call ladies 'Madam'. However, I suppose we have to deal with the Americans and their language difficulties."

The time I really remember about Mrs Shuckburgh, which makes me laugh even today, was when Evelyn, the scullery maid went out in the Courtyard to ring the lunch bell for the servants. She was standing at the foot of the stairs and when she rang the bell hardly a sound came out of it, the bell had been broken. She looked at me and said, "The bell's broken, how am I going to fetch everyone?" Mrs Shuckburgh was in the kitchen having her lunch. I looked at Evelyn and said, "I'll just open the door and whistle and they'll soon come running." Mrs Shuckburgh was taking no notice of our conversation, as I stepped to the door, put two fingers in my mouth and let out the most piercing of whistles, something I had learned to do when I was growing up in the East End. Mrs Shuckburgh turned white as a ghost and said, "What on earth is that dreadful sound?" I explained my whistling expertise to her as she stood with a look of disbelief on her face. She said, "Really Eileen, you sound like a street urchin. You must never do that in this house again." She then walked out of the kitchen, turned to me with a slight grin on her face and said, "Another talent of Eileen's we were not aware of." When we all sat down to lunch, we could hardly eat for the laughter of seeing her expression. I have to admit even today I can still whistle with the best.

One afternoon Mrs Shuckburgh was sitting at her writing desk, which faced the front windows of the house, next to the front door. She looked up and pressed up against the window was a big brown nose which belonged to Snowy, one of the horses. Snowy had apparently escaped from the stables, walked up the front steps and was just standing there staring at Mrs Shuckburgh. Mrs Shuckburgh went nuts, she flew into the pantry, saying, "Eileen, Eileen, do something, do something!" I said, "Do what?" She said, "Snowy is at the front door." I said, "What did he do, ring the front bell?" She was definitely not amused! She just kept shouting, "Do something." So I went and found Marie who always had an amazing way with animals. Marie slowly walked up the steps while speaking softly to Snowy. We were scared to death that Snowy would get spooked and fly off the front steps and break a leg, but as Marie quietly spoke to him, she got hold of his mane and slowly walked him down the steps. She was speaking so softly that we couldn't even hear what she was saying. But Snowy heard her. She walked him down the steps and back into the stables. Mrs Shuckburgh was so relieved. I told her that Snowy probably just wanted some afternoon tea. Again, Mrs Shuckburgh was not amused by my comment, but I thought it rather funny; to see a horse walking up the steps, ringing the door bell and asking for a cup of tea!

Years later, I took my two year old son, Keith, to visit the Brigadier, Mrs Gault and Mrs Shuckburgh at their home in Mt. Saint Hillarie in Canada. After we had eaten lunch, Mrs Shuckburgh commented about how lively Keith seemed to be and as, she reached out her hand to pat Keith on the head, he promptly bit her finger! She drew back in shock and said to no-one in particular, "Oh, what a rumbustious little boy, just like his mother when she was young."

Mrs Shuckburgh was a character even in her final years and she must have been the belle of the ball and the centre of much attention when she was young. She was someone, who in trying times during our stay at Hatch Court, made things a little less serious and a little more tolerable.

On Tuesdays, which was my day off, I would run down the drive, catch the bus into Taunton and go to the cinema to escape the utter dullness of the routine of day to day existence. At least a musical could take my mind off the war and the drabness of everyday life.

In the areas which surround Hatch Beauchamp, most of the villages are small farming communities. I was able to see that as I made my way around the countryside in 2010. The largest and certainly closest town of any note is the market town of Taunton, which is about five miles from Hatch. This seemed to provide the only sense of escape for someone like my mother who had grown up in London, which was the biggest city in the world at that time.

However, as the war progressed, Taunton became a centre of activity for soldiers from Canada, England, and the United States. It became far busier and much more exciting, but, as my mother recalled, "suddenly you had to be careful who you talked to."

One thing I have always remembered about being in Taunton was The Castle Hotel. I often passed there and saw the local 'gentry' coming and going, whether for drinks, dinner or a night of dancing. At first, I was resentful that these people seemed to be leading such a pleasant life, in the middle of a war, but as time went by I realized this was the life they had always led. Many of them saw no reason to change because of war and even with the influx of soldiers into Taunton, The Castle remained more of a place for officers, rather than the enlisted men.

When I watched the finely dressed ladies and men going in for an evening of enjoyment, I think it made me very jealous; not really of them, but because it wasn't me walking through the door. For the most part I blamed the war. It seemed when all else failed and you couldn't do what you wanted or get something you wanted, you blamed the war. I guess, in that sense, I was no different from anyone else in my situation.

The Castle Hotel was first opened in the late 18th Century as the Clarkes Hotel. It is a landmark in Taunton and reflects the beautiful style of architecture from that period. For over 50 years, the Hotel has been owned and operated by the Chapman family and is still a favourite venue for tourist and for 'special nights out'.

The Odeon Theatre was one of the most popular spots in town. It was here that Eileen escaped from the daily responsibilities of work and taking care of her brothers and sister. The Odeon was popular with everyone, both local inhabitants and Taunton's new residents who had arrived as a result of the war, because they showed mostly American films.

She saw 'Gone with the Wind' many times there, Bob Hope and Bing Crosby were starring in their Road pictures, and countless films of wartime love stories and romance were shown. Movies that inspired patriotic fever were always a hit….. although mom remembered soldiers being in the movie house when a certain General of the one of the armies was in the newsreels, and there was everything from shouts, to jeers, laughter or outright boos. It depended on who made up the audience how the movie was received.

She remembered one day watching the latest film, which was about Americans in the Pacific, shortly after the attack on Pearl Harbor. The British soldiers, who were watching, began catcalls and shouting comments such as 'The Americans are in the war, at last. But how good will they be at fighting?' It was difficult for people to understand that until Pearl Harbor, sentiment in the United States for sending their young men into combat was not popular. The Japanese changed the reluctance, on the part of America to fight, one Sunday morning in early December after the Japanese attacked Pearl Harbour.

Mom enjoyed films that were musicals. I truly believe my mother thought then she was one of the great undiscovered dancers of her time. I remember when growing up, she and my father danced a lot… and that they were pretty good! I guess that is why she would do just about anything to cajole Mrs Gault into letting her go to a dance in a nearby village.

By the middle of 1941 and into 1942 the war had began to become a strain on civilians. Rationing had begun to become a source of frustration.

One Sunday morning, we were told that clothes were to be rationed as of 'today' so there was no chance to run out and buy anything. We were given clothing coupons and I think we received about 26 coupons a year. A single dress was around 14 coupons and shoes were 7. So you can imagine how 'well dressed' we all were. We had our shoes repaired until the leather couldn't meet the upper part of the shoe. We wore shoes with wooden soles that opened in the middle when you bent your foot and in spite of stuffing my shoes with cardboard, they still weren't comfortable, so I spent seven precious coupons on a pair of silver shoes.

The blackout remained in effect and that caused the winter nights to be long and lacking in adventure, and the daily routine of work and looking after the boys and her sister began to take a toll on Eileen.

In October 1944, addition to her work at Hatch, and any war work she was required to do, she was assigned by the war office to work in the laundry in Taunton. She was to wash and fold sheets at the American Hospital for wounded soldiers returning from France. It was hard work, but better than her first job offer which was cleaning out railroad coaches at the Taunton train station. It was a hard and busy life for a girl of 16.

However, everyone was assigned work by the War Office when they turned 16, so as with many British people, she did what was required to help. There really was no option for healthy young women from all backgrounds.

One of the things about war work was it was expected and there was little choice in the job you were assigned. When they first told me I would be sweeping out train coaches, I remembered that I had ridden in trains before and had seen the condition they were in once vacated by soldiers. I was determined I was not going to do that and, of course, told them so. So, the disbursing officer in Taunton said, "Well dear, since that seems to be something you would not enjoy, perhaps I can assign you a job where you can learn a trade for later in life." His sarcasm was almost laughable but the joke was on me. Into the laundry I went. Working in the laundry was hard work and, although it was important to help the wounded soldiers, it was not something I particularly enjoyed. Hence, I did not become an owner of a laundry later in life. If the disbursing officer was out to teach me a lesson about my idea of wanting to choose a job, he succeeded.

As the Brigadier was in charge of the Canadian Holding Forces at Aldershot, people of note continued to arrive, to see him. One person who visited was Clive Benson of His Majesty's Government. He was the Brigadier's nephew.

Clive Benson had visited the house a number of times. He worked for the government and was attached to the Embassy in Portugal.

He had a somewhat dry sense of humour and talked about how he alone was holding together the overseas political dealings of the Churchill government, but he was always nice to the children. One weekend, we were in the back kitchen eating our dinner and he came in to return a plate. As he walked out he mentioned that there had been raids the night before in the Taunton and Chard areas. From the frequency of alerts in recent nights, the 'Hun' were starting nuisance raids again. Warnings had slackened somewhat in the last few months. I returned upstairs from my duties in the kitchen to the room I shared with Rosemary. It was a warm evening and I suggested to Rosemary that we should go out on the balcony that was above the first floor. She was always reluctant to do this because we were constantly getting caught by Mrs Gault or her mother.

Anyway we went out and watched the empty sky. You could almost always hear the sound of far off gunfire drifting over the fields. Whether it was Taunton, Wrantage, or somewhere nearby it became a part of our lives. On this particular night, as Rosemary and I talked on the balcony, a familiar sound of an airplane came from the right side of The Court, and just as she said, "What's that?" I looked up and a German bomber flew directly in front of the house. It was so close I felt I could have touched it. It was the well-known Dornier, a plane who almost everyone who had experienced a raid knew on sight. It was not bombing anything in the area, but it seemed to be looking at the house. One thing the war taught me was that your imagination can and does play tricks on you. I knew the bomber was not looking at the house, but I was always somewhat uneasy at The Court on bright moonlit nights. The house stands on a slight hill and on a clear night, it stood out like a beacon. I always wondered why it was not bombed or attacked.

When I visited Hatch Court in April of 2010, I spoke to a wonderful woman named Hazel Vernon, the Aunt of John Townson, and the same age as my mother. I asked her if she remembered my mother and she said, "Yes, she was the evacuee who was slim and pretty and a feisty one at that (a lot of people including her own family used that term when describing my mother during the war). I asked her why she thought Hatch Court had never been attacked during the war. She said, "Oh, but it was." She could not remember exactly when, but had spent much time at The Court and lived close by. She said, "One night the house was hit by machine gun fire from a passing German plane and if you look at the columns on the side of the front of the house, you can probably make out faded bullet holes." After our conversation, I walked to the front of the beautiful old house and there were the marks, somewhat faded from the almost seventy years that have passed, but they were there, right where she said they would be. I don't know where my mother was on the night the house was shot at, but apparently she had every reason to feel uneasy. Mr Benson was undoubtedly correct that the "Hun" were conducting nuisance raids in the area!

Everyday life as an evacuee was most certainly a very different life for me and, over the years, with the constant arrival of guests and visitors, was very exciting at times.

Chapter 9

Important Visitors

I have often wondered what made me start, not just learning about my mother's life during the war, but discovering everything I could about what transpired in those six years during 1939 to 1945. I had grown up hearing bits and pieces about her life and, although it was interesting, I never intended to spend five years trying to find out what her life was like on a daily basis during those years.

I think, however, the driving force in my desire to learn more, started in 1982 when I had just finished reading an excellent book by John Keegan, called 'Six Armies in Normandy'. In the prologue of Keegan's book, I ran across a number of names and places he referred to, which I had heard mentioned in conversations with my mother when she spoke about the war and her time living at Hatch Court.

Keegan, the son of an Inspector of Schools, grew up not very far from Taunton and its surrounding villages and the names and places he mentioned were places I had heard in my mother's stories. The more I read Keegan's book, names, such as Thornfalcon, Curry Mallet, Curry Rivel, Upottery, registered in my mind. Then I saw the name 'Hatch Beauchamp' and I definitely knew that name! When I showed John Keegan's book to my mother, she read the first part of his story as a boy during the war, handed the book back to me and said, *"We could very well have been neighbours."* I stood transfixed and asked, "Mom, do you know these places and the villages he is talking about?" *"Of course,"* she said, *"We used to go to dances in some of the villages. American paratroopers were at Upottery and I used to walk down Curry Mallet Road to see friends and go to school."* She then said, *"Many of the Officers and Generals, including a few members of Churchill's war cabinet, used to come to Hatch to see the Brigadier after they had been to visit their troops in those places he mentioned in his book."*

It was that statement, by my mother, that led me to ask her about her recollections of the now long-gone Generals, Air Chief Marshals, and two members of Sir Winston Churchill's war cabinet, who as my mother said *"Used to stop at Hatch Court to meet the Brigadier."* My mother wrote down the names of those men she recalled meeting, serving dinner to and, in a few cases, actually dancing with, including a Canadian officer and a British Air Marshal, whose gallantry and bearing have remained with my mother to this day.

During the Second World War, many of the officers of various Allied armies were a close knit group of men, who as a result of their careers, knew each other by name and reputation, if not through personal acquaintance. The British and Canadian senior officers had served together in the First World War and, in the years between wars, were often posted close to each other, in various duty stations. It was during this time that friendships and acquaintances were made that would become important and useful less than 25 years later. Not all these relationships were friendly, of course and, they were not without normal professional jealousies.

When my mother arrived at Hatch Court in 1939, she had never met, in her words *'people of importance'*, and was certainly unprepared for the notables she would meet and the events that would occur around her, during the coming years.

Shortly after the children were all settled in The Court and we became used to our new and different world of living in a small country village, I noticed that the friends of the Brigadier and Mrs Gault were no ordinary acquaintances. As I came home from school one day and walked up the long tree-lined drive to the main house, I saw a huge change from when I had taken the younger children to school that morning. Then things had been quiet and almost serene within Hatch.

I passed a few farmers along the road leading through the village and I remember seeing two British army trucks rumbling down the road heading to Taunton. Mrs Gault had already warned us to pay attention to the traffic when we were away from the house, as she had learned there would be a lot of army vehicles in the area in the coming days. I returned along Curry Mallet Road, which ran in front of Hatch Court and there was a line of trucks parked bumper to bumper winding the length of the long drive from the house to the road. Soldiers were everywhere. There were tents set up by the deer park and in the field adjacent to the main house. I gazed upon these men as they busily went about setting up their camp. The Brigadier was, at that time, dividing his days between Aldershot (The British Army's equivalent to West Point) and seemingly endless meetings with smartly dressed officers from both the British and Canadian Armies. It was then that I had my first experience of high-ranking officers, who would be a part of our lives for the next six years.

My mother did not know, at the time, but Great Britain was preparing for war on the European continent. The soldiers who had arrived at Hatch that day were members of one of the Empire's most famous regiments, the Royal Ulster Rifles.

When I walked to the house, a handsome young soldier, near the fence by the drive, snapped to attention, wishing me 'a good afternoon' and asked me my name. Stunned at this handsome young man's casual air, I said, "Eileen." He asked me, 'Do you live in the big house?' I replied, "Yes, I am an evacuee." He leaned over the fence, took off his beret and unpinned his RUL badge, which he handed to me and said, 'Here, now you will not forget me.'

I now have that long-forgotten soldier's beret badge of the Royal Ulster Rifles in my study. My mother said she saw him, from time to time, in the camp and the village over the next few months, but never knew his name. She remembered that when they left one day in early 1940, as suddenly as they had arrived, she asked Mrs Gault, *"Where have the Rifles gone?"* She responded rather sombrely, 'To France dear.'

She was told later by the Brigadier, that most of the men who had encamped on the grounds had been killed or taken prisoner by the Germans, in the battle for France the next summer, when the phoney war ended and the real war in Western Europe began.

Although war had been declared and men were training and preparing for battle all over England, little changed within the walls of Hatch Court.

Brigadier Gault had been recalled to active duty in 1939 by the Canadian Army. He had many friends, in both the British and Canadian armies, who came to the countryside whenever they could, to get away from the rigours of training troops, endless meetings, war games and the starched collar atmosphere of London.

Mrs Shuckburgh told me one day in early 1940, that a Canadian General was coming to see the Brigadier. Later that afternoon a car arrived at the front gate of the House. There were soldiers on the grounds and they stopped the car and shortly thereafter, waved it through to the main house. I was working as a parlour maid and happened to be in the front hall when there was a rather loud knock at the front door. Since I was the only one in the foyer, I went to the door and opened it. There stood this small framed man in what appeared to be old clothes and a cloth cap. He was a very non-descript looking person to me, as I was expecting a large man in a General's uniform. I asked him, in my most 'official' sounding voice, what he wanted and how could I help him? He looked rather taken aback and said, "I am here to see Hamilton Gault". Well in those days, few people referred to the Brigadier as Hamilton. Thinking he must be a tradesman, I told him to go around to the side of the house to the servants' entrance, and I would see if the Brigadier was available.

He looked rather startled and asked, "Where is the servants' entrance?" I pointed to the side of the house, and said, "Around the corner, through the area where the cars are parked and the horses are kept." He simply walked off and said, 'Tell the Colonel' (very few people ever referred to the Brigadier as Colonel, his WWI rank)'that Andrew McNaughton wishes to speak to him.' That should have told me something, but it didn't. I nodded and shut the front door; the front door was this massive, heavy oaken door that was obviously not designed for a girl of 13 to close easily.

Just as I shut the door, Mrs Shuckburgh came down the main stairwell. She asked, "Who was that Eileen"? I said, "I think it is a tradesman to see the Brigadier." She asked me, "Well, did he give his card or his name?" I said, "Yes, but I forgot what he said his name was." She looked out of the front window as this small man walked down the steps to the side of the house.

Well, I thought Mrs Shuckburgh would faint dead away in the hallway! She looked at me, her face took on an ashen colour, and she said, 'That is GENERAL ANDREW MCNAUGHTON!' I said, "Are you sure?" She almost shouted, "Eileen, he is General McNaughton, the head of the Canadian Army in England. Now go to the tradesmen's entrance and get him, now!'

I was speechless. I did not know who General McNaughton was, but being the Commander-in-Chief of the Canadian Forces 7th Corps, had to make him someone very important, even I knew that. So I flew through the house, ran to the side entrance, flung open the door and just as the General came around the corner, I mumbled, "I am so very sorry Sir, please do come in. I will take you immediately to the Brigadier and Mrs Gault." Being the gracious man that he was, he smiled and said, 'Thank you young lady,' and strode past me into the house. It is a wonder I was not sent to live in the wine *cellar for the duration. It was not the first or last time I would make such an error with visitors to Hatch.*

It would also not be the last time my mother saw General McNaughton at Hatch Court, as he and most of the top commanders of the Canadian Army, along with many of its officers, would visit Hatch numerous times in the three years prior to D-Day. Although my mother's primary dealings with these men and other notables whom she met, would be that as a maid and server of their meal, when the Gaults had one of their many dinner parties, she did have opportunities to speak to some of these visitors. In a few cases, by chance, she met their families, who had come from Canada to join their husbands during the war. The results, while always memorable to my mother, did not always make for a 'cracking' good time.

Once there was a treasure hunt arranged. Lots of children of the gentry came. We had to follow 'clues' all over the estate. I had to take Reggie Cutteram, one of the little evacuee boys and another boy called Gerald Sulous, whose father was with the British government. Gerald was an only child. We had just started out on our treasure hunt when Reggie fell down on our way to the farm. Gerald dragged him along the gravel, he so wanted to win, and Reggie tore his knee open. I hit Gerald hard and we quarrelled the whole time, and poor Reggie was crying with the blood running down his leg. Needless to say we didn't win, for which I was glad. We got back to the courtyard and Mrs Gault dressed Reggie's knee and asked what happened. I told her what had happened and Gerald just stood with a grin on his face.

    We later played a game on the lawn called Hatch Cricket. Everyone was there. I told Gerald I was going to bash his head in with the cricket bat for what he did to Reggie. Mrs Shuckburgh was horrified at my threat. I, however, did not bash his head in with the cricket bat, but I certainly thought about it. I could not bear the thought of us, (the evacuee children) being mistreated by anyone.

As was with anything in the life of evacuees; good, bad, indifferent or exciting, some events just became routine. My mother was in many ways a witness to history, whether as a result of her evacuation from London in 1939, or her experiences in London during the 'Blitz'. These moments of her life became part of what was then known among the people of Great Britain as 'getting on with it'. This was the life my mother led, she did not realise that the famous men and military officers, whose lives would later be described in history books, were the same people she was required to serve meals to while at Hatch Court.

Shortly before the Blitz began in earnest in 1940, I remember Mrs Gault calling all the servants and the 11 evacuees into the Long Room (a room we seldom entered, as it was an unspoken law that we were not to venture into certain parts of the Manor House) for a briefing.

An acquaintance of the Brigadier, from the First World War, was coming for the weekend with his wife and son. Major General George R. Pearkes VC, (General Pearkes had won the Victoria Cross in 1917, during the Battle of Passchendale in the Somme offensive) along with two British Colonels, would be 'resting' and dining at the Court on the following Friday. Mrs Gault explained to us that General Pearkes, his wife and son, John, were to be treated with the utmost courtesy as he was famous and a brave officer currently serving as commander of the 2nd Canadian Division. His wife was, we were told, a wonderful lady. Their son, John, who was my age of 13, was a nice enough lad, but was somewhat unruly. We were told to be on our best behaviour. What a weekend it turned out to be for me, Dennis and Charles.

During their stay, John was always outside when we came home from school. He was either telling Hancock, the groom, to get a horse ready for him to ride, or walking around dressed in his kilt of the Canadian Black Watch. He was a spoilt little boy. One day, in particular, as we came in the front gate, John was standing there with a huge bar of Cadbury's chocolate. The little boys watched him as he ate two squares of chocolate and then threw the rest into the bushes. I was so mad, I flew into the bushes, found it, wiped it off and shared it with the boys. We couldn't buy any sweets at the village shop. The man who owned it wouldn't sell us anything for he saved it for the local kids. We were still considered 'outsiders'. One day John Pearkes hit my brother Dennis across the face. I waited until we were all in the park, then he and I had a terrible knock-down battle. He never hit any of the little boys again.

Lots of Canadian soldiers came to Hatch and we rehearsed all kinds of little plays, skits and songs at night in the mess hall. Usually on Sunday afternoons, we then filed into the drawing room and performed for all the guests. We always ended our performances by waving maple leaves, from the beautiful maple trees which the Brigadier had brought from Canada and planted in the deer park and singing 'The Maple Leaf Forever'. It brought the house down and I know the Canadians just loved it.

When the Brigadier was released from the Canadian forces because of his accident, he came back to live at Hatch full time. As he was no longer dividing his time between Aldershot and Hatch, life at Hatch changed as more serious events and discussions took place. There was a commando raid in Norway and it involved some Canadian troops. A few weeks after that, Major General Potts, who was in command of the ill-fated Canadian commando raid at Dieppe, came to visit the Brigadier. They spent hours in the study and no-one was allowed to disturb them. General Potts was, at the time, the Commander of the 2nd Canadian Infantry Brigade, Saskatoon Light Infantry.

The Brigadier was at Hatch most of the time in September 1941. He had fallen while in the Army and broken the stump of his leg, after previously losing his leg in WWI in one of the many battles in which he participated. It was a very trying time as he did not adapt well to being removed from action with the troops. He brought his batman, Burleigh, with him to help him, but it wasn't long before Mrs Gault tried to turn him into a servant, so Burleigh returned to Aldershot and the PPCLI.

Early in the war, Royal Naval Commander Ingram (he was from South Africa) came to visit and stayed with us for about a week. He was much decorated as he had rammed a U-Boat and sunk it. Later, his ship was torpedoed and sank, but luckily he survived. Before being rescued, he drifted at sea surrounded by cases of rum, and tearfully he watched as the cases sank. He used to tell the young boys many stories of being at sea.

Whilst my mother was living at Hatch Court, in early 1942, two of the most important men in England arrived. Many officers from various armies passed through, but none were as renowned as two gentlemen, from London, who arrived one night for dinner. Whispered conversations were common place during those years, both in the hallways and outside the Brigadier's study between the Brigadier and his wife. My mother and the other servants went about their everyday duties and paid little attention to the comings and goings of Hatch Court's visitors. After all, servants and evacuees were not a part of the family. However, each day was rarely just a normal day, as the Brigadier received so many important guests.

One day, Dennis came into the kitchen when I was polishing silverware. As we had no real silverware in our house on Libra Road I was not used to, nor did I enjoy, the polishing duties. It simply added more work to the many afternoon responsibilities the two other maids and I carried out each day. Dennis ran up to me and said, "Eileen, I just heard Mrs Gault say to Durman (the chauffer and butler) that she and the Brigadier were expecting two very important visitors tomorrow for dinner, and she asked Durman to brush down the Brigadier's dress uniform."

(I think Dennis, more so than Charles, was always in awe of the Brigadier. When Dennis grew older I always felt he tried to pattern himself on the Brigadier). So, whoever they were they must be important or there would not be so much 'to do'. As Dennis was nine, anyone in uniform was important to him and both my brothers were always very excited when 'soldiers' came. They loved to stare at these men and would hide in the hallways to steal a look at any officer who arrived. I said to him, "Who are these important visitors?" He didn't know, but he was excited nonetheless. With that he flew out of the back door into the stable area to find Charles, to share his news with him and the other boys. I shook my head and went back to polishing silver. I promised myself in those days that when I got older I would never polish another piece of silver in my life. Keeping the house clean and polishing pieces of silver seemed endless tasks, with little time left for anything else.

Shortly after my brother's frantic trip through the kitchen, Mrs Gault informed Rogers of a special menu for later in the week. Even though the Gaults, like everyone else, had to change their lifestyle and dining habits during the war, Hatch Court always seemed able to obtain excellent food and drink when guests were in residence. The Brigadier was a familiar figure in the area and was treated with great respect by local farmers, butchers and tradesmen, who knew him well. While not always able to obtain pre-war extravagances, seldom did the dining table of Hatch Court go without. Instructions were given that Rosemary and I would assist Rogers in serving the meal and Durman would function as the Head of staff. I believe it was a Thursday or Friday when two cars slowly pulled into the drive and parked slightly away from the main door. Normally, anyone who came to the Court in those days pulled right up to the front door, and in most cases made a show of getting their belongings out of the car and if servants were with them, they scurried about to ensure their employers were let out of the car properly and were assisted in walking up the three steps to the main house.

It was all quite silly in my eyes as I felt few of the many visitors who arrived at Hatch, warranted such fuss. Actually, looking back on it, many of the very important men who arrived, did so with little or no fanfare. To me, it was always the lesser the rank, the bigger the production. Of course, in those days I always kept such opinions to myself, not that my opinion was ever sought on such matters. My problem was I was apt to give my opinion on matters on which I really should have remained silent.

Anyway, the cars I referred to pulled slowly to the side of the drive away from the entrance. As I was again cleaning silver in the front room, I looked out of the window and saw what struck me immediately as a pair of mismatched men; a slightly smaller older man walking next to a taller man with a head of unruly red hair. Whoever they were, if anything they looked quite lost. Two other men stepped out of the first car and looked around and lit up cigarettes. The men talked among themselves and walked casually up the front steps to the front door.

As there was a loud knock at the front door, I walked from the front room to the main hall and pulled open the heavy oak door. The tall red haired man spoke to me in an offhand manner and said, "Brigadier Gault please." As they both appeared rather nondescript from my point of view, I asked if they had an appointment with him. He looked rather taken aback, and the much shorter older man said, "Well yes, I suppose we do. Go and get him if you don't mind." The way he spoke dripped with sarcasm. I looked at them both and said, "Wait here," and closed the door.

I knocked on the Brigadier's study and Mrs Gault opened the door. I said, "Mrs Gault, there appear to be two tradesmen at the door, here to see the Brigadier." She asked if I had asked their names. I said, "No, they are waiting outside." She walked past me to the front door as the Brigadier rose from behind his desk and said, "You know Eileen, you should always ask whoever comes to the front door their names." With that he said, "No matter, let's see who has come and what their business is."

As I turned around Mrs Gault was at the front door and the two gentlemen were now inside the house. She looked at me, then focused her attention on the, as of yet, unnamed strangers. She said, "Hammie, (the way she always addressed the Brigadier) Lord Beaverbrook and Brendan Bracken have arrived." I stared with mouth open at England's Minister of Information, Brendan Bracken. He was Winston Churchill's right hand man, in fact he was more like a son. The other gentleman was the Minister of War Production, Lord Beaverbrook. Lord Beaverbrook was a Canadian and a friend of the Brigadier before the war. I was much in awe of them as their names were well known and familiar to almost everyone in England.

As they walked past me, I walked quickly through the front rooms to the kitchen to tell my friend, Rosemary, we would be serving dinner to two members of the Prime Minister's War Cabinet. Little did I know how much fun Rosemary and I would have serving dinner to these famous guests. Even though we had very important visitors regular duties were performed as usual, and my brothers and sister went to their normal lessons at the local Hatch Beauchamp School.

When dinner time arrived, which was at about 8.00pm, Rosemary, Rogers and I prepared to serve the evening meal. As we began serving dinner to these two famous men and Mrs Gault and the Brigadier, I thought to myself how unbelievable that I was part of the staff who were about to fill the soup bowls of Lord Beaverbrook and Minister Bracken.

For some strange reason, I don't know why, I decided to 'liven up our duties'. As I was standing behind Brendan Bracken, I caught the eye of Rosemary. Now you must realise I spent a good deal of time with her and she was great fun to be with, but she was always afraid, when called upon to serve dinner, she would as she said 'muck it up'. Well, as I ladled the soup into the bowls, I was positioned directly behind the guests and Rosemary was on the other side of the table placing bread on the side plates, when I caught her eye and made the silliest face I could think of. I had the ability to grin and then in a flash appear very serious. Rosemary saw me, began to giggle and then to laugh.

The dinner conversation became rather quiet as Mrs Gault looked at her and said, "Is there something you find amusing Rosemary?" She turned as white as a ghost. She said, "No Madam," and quickly went into the main kitchen. I, of course, kept a serious look and said, "Will there be anything else Madam?" Mrs Gault seemed to be aware something had happened, and as I was always somewhat the 'rebel' of the evacuees, she said in a rather stern voice, "That will be all Eileen." I bowed slightly, as was required of us, and walked silently into the main kitchen. Rosemary and I burst into laughter and when asked by Rogers what we found so amusing we simply said nothing. He wouldn't have understood. It was just a joke between the two of us. After dinner, the Brigadier, Lord Beaverbrook and Brendon Bracken retired to the study. With the door closed, a sudden silence descended over the front of the house. Mrs Gault went into the long room and spoke with her mother, Mrs Shuckburgh. As we cleared away the dishes and proceeded to reset the dining room place settings, one of the men I had seen earlier in the day, who had driven the car of Lord Beaverbrook, came into the dining room. He quietly asked, "May I have a cup of tea?" I said, "Yes sir," and went to the kitchen to fetch it. I learned later, from one of the soldiers in the grounds, that he was an armed protection officer of the ministers. It made that night even more exciting and memorable.

I think everyone knew I had done something to encourage Rosemary's behaviour, but they didn't know quite what. We had to make our own fun. With all that was happening around us, it was the little amusing things that kept us going. We did, sometimes behave like children, and hopefully, at times, it reminded others we were still only young girls, which, in fact, we were.

The war had made us grow up fast. Serving dinners was work and I felt if we didn't keep our sense of humour, we would all go mad! Of course, not everyone agreed with my attitude, and from time to time I was called 'up the carpet' for a 'discussion' with Mrs Gault in private about my behaviour. This seemed to be an ongoing problem for both Mrs Gault and me, but I never stopped doing these little things.

In 1943, it seemed many more people came to Hatch to meet the Brigadier. By then he had retired due to an accident, but that did not slow down the continuous flow of visitors who wanted to see him and Mrs Gault.

We, or the Barnett children as we were known around the village, were the only evacuees left at Hatch Court and the house seemed bigger and with fewer people around, we were even more lonely.

Whilst a number of servants had come and gone, some to war, some to other jobs closer to their families, we had nowhere to go. My father remained in London and, due to his long working hours, there was not much chance of a real life at home with him. Since I had left school and was working in Taunton in war service and still doing my servant's duties at Hatch, we remained away from home and my brothers and sister continued to attend school in Hatch Beauchamp. Mrs Gault, however, was determined to continue to maintain the 'Hatch Spirit', as she called it. With the constant flow of officers and dignitaries coming to The Court, life at the house continued as before, and even with war all around us, dinner parties, although somehow unreal, were a regular event.

It is not with any bitterness I say this, it just seemed strange with war reports of battles, bombings and the rumours of the coming of the Yanks, sometimes a dinner party seemed out of place. With that said, it always broke the monotony of my life and did give even a maid something to look forward to. After all, there were no new clothes, coupons for everything, rationed food and constantly being told what to do, when to be there, how to behave and even what to say. As a young girl, I wanted to go to dances, visit Taunton and go to movies. Sometimes I would see soldiers in the village, primarily Canadians, some Americans but mostly British. They all looked so handsome, I longed to meet one or at least talk to someone whose life was as different from mine as being on the moon.

So in the first week of May 1943 when Mrs Gault called me into the long room to tell me there was to be a dinner on Wednesday night for an important Royal Air Force Officer and three of his staff members, I was somewhat excited. Although I wasn't exactly sure of the importance of an Air Chief Marshal, he must have a high rank to be having dinner at Hatch Court. Mrs Gault said he would arrive at exactly 6.00pm; punctuality had always been an English tradition. Dinner would be at 8.00, after he and the Brigadier had held a meeting behind the doors of the 'mysterious' study. I say 'mysterious', only because we were told from the day we arrived, never to go into the study unless called.

Since I would be helping to serve dinner with the other parlour maid, Joan, along with Rogers, as usual my curiosity got the better of me. I asked Mrs Gault, "Madam who will be coming to dinner?" She stood silently, for what seemed like an eternity, and looked at me with disbelief, "I will check with the Brigadier and ask him if he feels you should be told who will be joining us". Naturally my face turned as red as my sweater and I apologised for asking such a forward question. Mrs Gault turned on her heel and walked out of the room without a word.

I found it difficult to understand two simple things at the age of 16. One, there were always security concerns about who came and went at Hatch Court. Two, it was really none of my business and that was the point I always seemed to forget. Mrs Gault and Rogers did their best to make me understand that, for six long years.

Nonetheless, Wednesday arrived and the house looked magnificent, as it did every night, even during the blackout. The inside of the House with its walls of paintings that I thought would look in their natural place if they were in a museum, china plates that you could see your face in and crystal glasses that reflected the candlelight like diamonds in a mirror. That was Hatch Court in the war years, still reflecting the beauty of a time past and a time that would soon be forgotten by many. For the dinner being given for Air

Chief Marshal Sir Philip Joubert de la Ferte, Commander-in-Chief of the Royal Air Force Coastal Command, everything would look its glittering best. I, along with the other two housemaids, served dinner as instructed at precisely 8.00pm. Although the routine of working, keeping an eye on my brothers and sister and my duties at Hatch were tiresome, every once in a while, something occurred that made the war seem so distant and life, at least for a day, a Cinderella kind of event. This evening would prove to be one of those magical experiences, although it lasted only for a few precious minutes.

After dinner was over the Gaults, Air Chief Marshal Joubert and the two British officers retired to the Long Room for brandy and sherry. I was in the dining room helping Rogers clear up the dishes and taking them into the kitchen to be washed by Marie, who at that time was functioning as a scullery maid, not the most glamorous of assignments. As we worked in the kitchen, Mrs Gault appeared and asked if someone would bring in an ashtray, so that the officers could enjoy an evening cigar. Rogers nodded to me and said, "Eileen take the ashtray to the Brigadier." I placed the ashtray on a silver tray (you didn't just carry an ashtray, you presented it) and walked down the hall to the Long Room. As I entered the room and set the ashtray down on a table beside the Brigadier, I bowed slightly and turned to leave. It was then I heard the most beautiful piano music I'd ever heard.

Apparently, one of the British officers was an exceptional pianist. He was playing classical pieces when the Air Chief Marshal said, "Play something upbeat we can all enjoy". I backed out and was standing, half peering into the room, listening to this young officer's beautiful sounds. He was playing a piece which I had heard before, a waltz. I do not recall the name of the song, but I remember it was a waltz and for a moment I let my mind put me on a dance floor with some dashing soldier waltzing around the floor.

Suddenly, I realized I was being watched. Mrs Gault said, "Thank you Eileen that will be all." As I turned to go I heard this deep voice say, "Perhaps the young lady would like to waltz." I turned as red as a beetroot and said, "I don't know how to waltz," although I loved the music the officer played. At that moment, Air Chief Marshal Philip Joubert *stood up, walked towards me and said, "I will waltz with you my dear." I was speechless and stammered something like, "No thank you sir."*

I felt like crawling under the table, I was so embarrassed, but he said in a kind reassuring voice, "No matter, simply stand on my boots and I will teach you." I looked at the Brigadier, he always being the kindest of men said, "Go on then Eileen, dance with the officer." I looked at Mrs Gault who did not have quite the same kind expression as her husband, but nodded nonetheless. I walked over, looked at this giant of a man in a uniform that was as crisply pressed as anything I had ever seen and stepped up on his boots and he took my hands in his and around the floor we went.

After a few fleeting moments I stepped down off his boots and said, "Thank you sir." He smiled and said, "See, it is not difficult at all." I literally floated out of the room. Not only had I actually danced, I had entered into the long room and for a moment felt like a real person, not an evacuee from the East End. For that reason I will always remember my first waltz.

Sir Philip Joubert de la Ferte was born May 1887 and died January 1965. He was Air Chief Marshal Royal Air Force. He joined the Royal Field artillery in 1907, then transferred to the Royal Flying Corps in 1914. By the end of the war in 1918, he was Commander of the Royal Air Force in Italy. At the beginning of the Second World War, after a stint in India, he returned to Britain and was named Air Officer Commander-in-Chief, Coastal Command from 1941 to 1943. He was awarded the KCOB, Companion of the Order of St Michael and St George, DSO, MD (5 times). My mother later asked the Air Chief Marshal if he would be so kind as to sign her autograph book. I have that autograph proudly framed in my study today.

From time to time, Colonel Jimmy Gault and his wife came to Hatch and stayed for a few days. He was the Brigadier's cousin but nothing like the Brigadier. When the Brigadier was at Aldershot, it was decided that Mrs Gault would go and live in Colonel Gault's house and then the Col. and Mrs Gault would spend time at Hatch. Mrs Jimmy Gault brought her own lady's maid, Mabel, with her. So another event began.

Jimmy Gault was born June 26, 1902. He joined the Scots Guards in 1939 and served in WWII from 1939 – 1945 in the Middle East, North Africa, Sicily, Italy and N.W. Europe. He was promoted to Colonel in 1944. Awards: KCMG 1952; MVO 1943; OBE 1946 (MBE 1941). When General Eisenhower was Supreme Allied Commander in Europe, Jimmy Gault served as his British ADC. He was promoted to Brigadier in 1950 and Knighted in 1952. He died in January 1977.

Mabel didn't sleep with us on the top landing. She slept in Mrs Jimmy Gault's dressing room. On the first Sunday, she came into the kitchen for Mrs Gault's breakfast tray. She wanted a boiled egg (we were allowed 1 egg a month), toast, marmalade and coffee. Rosemary boiled the egg and put it in an egg cup. Mabel took the tray upstairs and came back right away and said, "This is not a 3 minute egg, Mrs Gault can't eat it." Rosemary cooked another one and that one came back as overcooked. Three eggs that wretched woman complained about.

By that time I was very angry. Then Mable came back down and said, "Mrs Gault would like some biscuits." I told her we didn't have any and if Mrs Gault wanted biscuits, she would have to bring her own. With that, Mable walked into the pantry and proceeded to take all the Sunday newspapers. The front of the house received the Sunday Times and Sunday Pictorial. We were allowed The People and The News of the World. I asked her where she was going with ALL the papers, and she replied "I am taking them to Mrs Gault." I said, "No, leave our papers, you can take the rest." She said "Oh, but Mrs Gault likes to read all the newspapers." I said, "Not today, you can have them after we have read them."

I had put some damp clothes in the airing cupboard. There were actually two airing cupboards on the top landing, and we were allowed to put our clothes in there if they weren't completely dried. The next thing I knew, when I went upstairs, all of my things were lying on the floor. I was livid and, of course, Mable had put all Mrs Jimmy Gault's clothes in there. I flew around the house and asked her what she thought she was doing. In the meantime, I put her clothes on the floor and mine back in the airing cupboard.

Fortunately, they all left soon afterwards and went back to where they came from and Mrs Hamilton Gault came home.

Needless to say, all hell broke loose and I was called to her bedroom at once. I think that carpet, to which I was so often called, must have been threadbare by the time I returned to London. I was 'dressed down', had the 'riot act' read to me.

I found it humiliating to be treated as though I was nothing by the servants of people who came to see the Brigadier and Mrs Gault. Working at Hatch Court was my job and I could not expect Mrs Gault to know everything that went on with maids, butlers, etc., but behind the scenes I felt it was my place to defend myself from these pompous people who, because of whom they worked for, thought they were something special. The officers, diplomats, ladies and, of course, the Brigadier and Mrs Gault, always treated us in a much kinder way than the people who worked for the visitors to the Court.

Anyway, Jimmy Gault and his wife came back time and again, but in future they always brought their own biscuits.

One experience that stood out in my mother's memory was as a result of a memorable phone call in 1943, which she took while working in the front parlour. I became aware of it in a throw-away comment during a conversation we had when I was in University in Oklahoma in the 1970s. I mentioned to her that I had just finished reading a book called 'My Three Years with Eisenhower', by Commander Harry Butcher, Eisenhower's American Naval Aide during the Second World War.

I said, "Mom, you should read this book about Eisenhower. He really used to 'read the riot act' to people when they failed to deliver on their responsibilities. He must have been some kind of man." She turned round and said, "*I know about General Eisenhower's reputation. I remember when he called one day to Hatch to talk to Colonel Jimmie Gault. I could tell from his voice when I answered the phone that he was not happy and he wanted to talk to Colonel Gault immediately, on what I gathered had to be something important.*"

She headed into the dining room with me trailing less than one step behind her. I said, "Mom wait a darn minute, YOU spoke to General Eisenhower, 'THE' General Eisenhower'?" She said, "*Yes, I have always remembered that call, it was so exciting for me just to hear his voice.*" Trying to keep my composure, I said "Well mom, if you have a minute would you mind telling me about the call."

Colonel Gault had arrived at Hatch from London on the Friday evening. He had injured his arm in a riding accident and had come to Hatch to recuperate. He spent Saturday morning with the Brigadier and retired to his room in the afternoon to rest. Mrs Gault had informed the staff that Colonel Gault was not to be disturbed for any reason.

As we prepared the dining room for the evening meal, I was passing through the main hall when the telephone rang. One of my duties was to answer the telephone as quickly as possible when it rang, so I stopped, picked up the receiver and said, "Hatch Beauchamp 225."

A very American sounding voice, with a hint of what I sensed to be impatience, said, "I need to speak to Colonel Jimmy Gault, please put him on the line." I replied, "I am sorry sir, but Colonel Gault is resting from a riding accident and left instructions he was not to be disturbed." Before I could even say, "May I take a message?" a sharp reply came firing back, "I am not interested in what Colonel Gault's instructions were, you tell him this is Eisenhower, General Eisenhower, and I want to speak with him now!" For what seemed like an eternity, I stood with the receiver in my hand as it registered with me that on the other end of the telephone was General Eisenhower, Commander-in-Chief of the U.S. Army in England. I may have been only 16, but everyone knew who Eisenhower was. I stammered and said, "I will get Colonel Gault right away General." With my hand shaking, I gently put down the receiver and flew upstairs to summon Colonel Gault.

I reached the second landing, ran down the hallway past Mrs Shuckburgh who said, "Eileen, you must not run in the house, always remember to walk." At least, I think that's what she said, as I was past her in a flash. Out of breath, I knocked rather firmly on the bedroom door. A moment later, a very annoyed Colonel Gault appeared and said, "What is it? I left instructions not to be disturbed." I said, "Yes, Colonel Gault I know, but there is a rather important call for you." He said, "Well, who is it then?" My moment had arrived. I looked at him and in my most grown up voice and manner said, "General Eisenhower". The Colonel's face went pale and his annoyed manner was gone. He looked at me and said he would be there immediately. In an instant, he appeared in his uniform tunic and quickly descended the stairs. Normally, I would have finished setting the table, but I slowly followed him down the stairs and pretended I was tidying up the sideboard, which was right next to the telephone. This was, after all, General Eisenhower. To say I wanted to overhear a bit of conversation was an understatement.

Colonel Gault picked up the receiver, took a deep breath and said, "Yes General, Gault here", and began to explain his riding accident. Eisenhower's voice boomed from the phone and cut him off by saying, "I don't give a damn what's wrong Jimmy, get back to Headquarters in London now!" Colonel Gault said simply, "Yes General, I will leave straight away", and he hung up.

As he turned, he looked at me and said, "Please tell the Brigadier I shall be leaving immediately for London and shall not be joining him and Dorothy for dinner." And with that he went up the stairs to gather his things.

I have remembered that phone call all my life and I still get the shivers knowing I had the honour of speaking to this legendary figure of WWII. Years later, after I became a U.S. citizen and had the opportunity to cast a vote in the presidential election of 1952, I proudly cast that vote for the man who I had spoken to, ever so briefly, on that day in 1943, Dwight D. Eisenhower.

In the autumn of 1943, as the village was full of British, Canadian, and the newly arrived American troops I was trying my best to convince Mrs Gault that I had to go to the dance at the village hall the next night. Of course, she said, "No", as again no-one was allowed to leave the grounds. I did not know who was coming or why we were being, as I used to tell the others, banished to the tower. But Mrs Gault was always fair and kind to us, so along with the other children (I of course did not consider myself a child at the worldly age of almost seventeen) I reluctantly agreed.

However, I crawled out of the upper window landing to see if I could catch a glimpse of this latest visitor, but Mrs Shuckburgh discovered me, as I was standing looking out over the grounds, and quickly put an end to my adventure. I was quickly brought inside, and whoever it was who came to the house that rainy autumn evening has to this day remained a mystery. One of the Princess Patricia's officers who was at *the Court that week later told me that a gentleman, who had arrived in a large car, had walked out to the deer park (which was directly in front of the main house) draped in a dark cape and stood silently in the light rain gazing up at the planes overhead, as they made their way to Germany from the nearby American base of Merryfield, which was about 4 miles from Hatch Beauchamp.*

The officer told me that one of the junior officers came out of the house and, at the urging of his fellow soldiers, walked up behind the solitary figure and said, "Don't you know you should at least have an umbrella if you intend to stand out here getting wet?" I was told that the man turned slowly to the young officer, lowered the cape from around his shoulders, and said, "My name is Churchill. What, young man is yours?"

One of the great things about Hatch Court was there was often an air of excitement to the House. I have no idea if what I heard about Winston Churchill being in front of the house that evening was true. I was never able to get anyone to confirm if he had been there. I like to think it was the famous man, who we all thought had saved England. Like many things that happened at Hatch over those years the truth will now probably remain hidden.

Although I have not been able to confirm whether it was the famous Prime Minister, but, as Churchill had known Brigadier Gault from Gault's time in the House of Commons, in the 1920s and 30s, and as Gault's role with the Canadian Army at the war's outset involved him in high level meetings with Allied Officers, it does seem very likely that it was the great man himself. It is doubtful that with the passage of the years we shall have little chance of discovering the truth.

I remember in late 1943, and again later in 1944, all the evacuees were required to remain in the Clock Tower (behind the main House) and were instructed by Mrs Gault under no circumstances were they to leave their rooms. Of course, my brothers and my sister Marie were quick to promise they would remain where they were told. On the other hand me being a little older and curious (or overly curious as I had been told many times before) I wondered why we should have to remain virtual prisoners for the evening, at least that is how I viewed it. You see young people seem to have a built in reluctance to do what they are told not to do and as a young girl I was no exception.

The day went by, as most days did, preparing dinner with Rogers, and the endless cleaning. I do not even remember now what Rosemary and I were cleaning, but there was always work to be done. After all we were getting paid for following our instructions.

This particular afternoon, an American jeep and American staff car pulled up at the front of the house. I believed all American officers travelled in large Cadillacs. That was not true, but whenever I went to Taunton, there were numerous large American staff cars racing around town. As I was putting the dinnerware on the dining room table, I looked out of the window and saw a car sitting in the main drive. It had three stars fluttering from its bumper, and beside it stood an American soldier casually talking to the men in the jeep. Mrs Gault came past the dining room, saw me and said, "Eileen, I thought I made it clear, everyone was to remain in the Clock Tower." I said, "Yes Madam," and hurried off.

I did not know who this General was, but, again, my curiosity got the better of me, so I asked, Jasper Durham, the chauffeur, "Who does the car belong to?" He looked at me and said, "I am sure if Mrs Gault or the Brigadier wanted you to know, they would have informed you." I never did find out, but learnt later, from some Yanks in the village, that BIG BRASS had been at the house the previous day, meeting the Canadian officers who were staying at Hatch.

Whilst researching the two events my mother refers to about the unknown visitors to Hatch, I discovered that on March 18th 1944 General Dwight D. Eisenhower landed in the Taunton area at RAF Culmhead in the late afternoon. The official reason for his presence that day was he was on an informal visit to a fellow General in the area. Records show he flew back to London the next day. This is verified in the excellent book 'Somerset at War' by Mac Hawkins, published in 1988. General Omar Bradley of the U.S. Army, who was one of the ground Force commanders in the D-Day landings, was a three star General whose name has appeared in various books connecting him to the Taunton area at the time of the build up to the invasion.

In reading a guest book, that John Townson shared with me in April 2010, of visitors to Hatch Court during the war years, I was amazed at the names I saw. Stanley Baldwin, a former British Prime Minister, Kay Chidwinton, who worked with the British House of Commons, was at Hatch in October 1941, and Canadian Major General F.F. Worthington, who was at the house in November 1943. He was better known to his fellow officers as 'Worthy' or 'Fighting Frank', and to this day is considered the father of the Royal Canadian Armoured Corps. This decorated soldier fought in the Canadian Army in the First World War and went on to develop the first Canadian Armoured Units for the Canadian Army in World War II. He is remembered today in Canada, in the province of Ottawa, by the Major General FF Worthington Park and tank museum. He died in 1967. Other visitors included a member of H.M. government from Lisbon, Mr. Clive Benson who was a frequent visitor to Hatch.

On asking my mother if she remembered any of these well known people, she replied that she might have served them a meal or delivered a drink to them, but as she has often reminded me so many people came to Hatch that unless she was told who they were she could not possibly recall the names of everyone who came.

Time has erased the names of many people of note from her mind, but she had two final stories of visitors she did remember coming to the House, who had a shroud of mystery forever wrapped around their visit. In talking to both my uncles before their deaths, they did remember two unnamed visitors and the circumstances surrounding their short visit to Hatch Court.

As I think back during those times, it is hard even for me to believe that I actually had the honour and privilege of meeting so many important men; the famous, the well known political figures, the brilliant officers, and all the others. They were experiences that I shall always treasure despite the underlying reason for those visits.

Dillington Hall

Gravestone of Brigadier A, Hamilton Gault and his wife Dorothy at St John's Chuch, Hatch Beauchamp

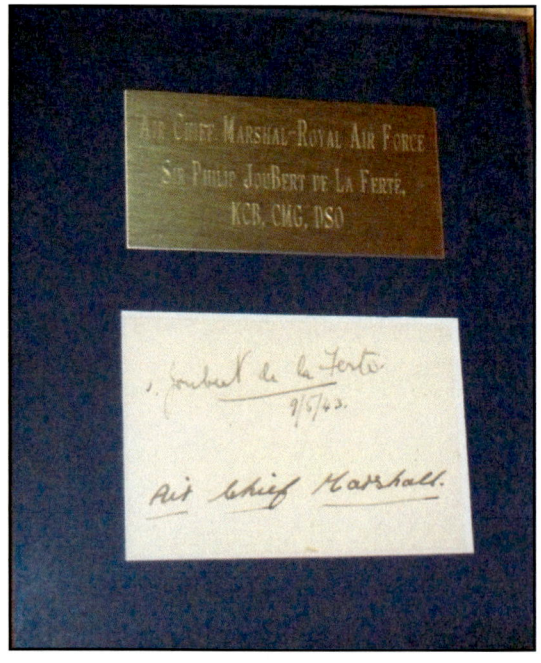

Autograph of Sir Philip Joubert de La Ferte with whom Eileen danced

Chapter 10

Moments of Sadness

I often thought during the six years that my brothers, sister and I spent at Hatch Court, how different our lives would have been had fate not placed us in the hands of Brigadier and Mrs Gault. So many children who were evacuated, had very difficult times at the hands of the people with whom they were placed. Some of these people should not have been left responsible for these poor children in their care. Our lives were difficult at times; no child ever forgets being parted from its parents at such a young age, but, for the most part, our new life was fairly comfortable and safe, and such a world apart from how we had lived, that each day seemed to bring new and interesting experiences.

We were not immune, however, from those moments of sadness that come with war and to the many other difficulties of life which we all faced. No-one I knew had an idyllic life and the tragedies of the war were always just around the corner. There were times of grief, and there were many events that made life difficult for an evacuee my age. Although I have pushed things to the back of my mind, many of the experiences still remain clearly in my memory and I remember them as though it were yesterday.

I remember the train station the day we left London; how my brothers cried and my sister was repeatedly sick. The fear of being told I was to be separated from my brothers still sends a feeling of dread through me. Two of the children, Julie 8 and her brother, Tubby 5, were evacuated with us and we spent our first year at Hatch together before they returned home to London, because they missed their parents so desperately. They lived not far from us in the East End and, as the Blitz intensified, they were killed during an air raid. An eight year old little girl and her five year old brother, lost so terribly. They were our friends, fellow evacuees and I always felt sad when I thought of their beautiful faces and sweet smiles. I have, for many years, had a picture, beside my bed, of them next to us and the other *evacuees and Mrs Gault, taken shortly after our arrival at Hatch. Their death was such a tragedy and so senseless.*

My mother related many stories about the not-so-pleasant times she experienced during that six years. Many renowned people and high-ranking officers came through Hatch in those years. For various reasons, some of which were cloaked in secrecy and we shall never know many who my mother served at dinner, while they were guests of the Gaults. Some of these people went on to achieve even higher military rank in the future, one became an author of some note, another guest at Hatch Court became the Governor General of British Columbia and one was on the staff at NATO after the war. Many received high decorations for their accomplishments and some were even knighted by King George VI. What she remembered, however, were the many soldiers of the armies from France, Canada, Poland, Britain and the United States she knew or has forgotten, and who did not live to see the end of the war. They were lost to history perhaps, but still remained in my mother's and their families' memory.

One evening in May 1940, while the battle for France still raged across the Channel, Brigadier and Mrs Gault drove their Bentley down the long drive, turned into Curry Mallet Road and then pulled into the field. Curry Mallet Road ran in front of the house and the field could be seen from the windows. All the children went to those windows and watched as a small plane landed roughly and taxied to a stop. The Bentley pulled up close to the little plane. Two people, a man in uniform and a lady, climbed awkwardly out of the aircraft and spoke to the Gaults for a short time, before the four people embraced and held each other for a long time. The officer and the woman then got into the plane, taxied down the field and lifted slowly into the failing summer light. Only moments later, as the Brigadier and Mrs Gault stood waving goodbye until the plane was out of sight. The Gaults then got into the Bentley and ever so slowly, it seemed, returned to the house.

As the car pulled into the drive, the children stood and watched as Mrs Gault, with tears streaming down her cheeks, walked silently passed them into the front hall. One of the little boys asked the Brigadier who the people were and where they were going? Quietly, the man who was so familiar with war, said to the boy, "They are dear friends and they are going back to France." My mother said she never found out who they were, but, they never returned to Hatch Court. A moment she never forgot about people she never even knew.

The Gaults had many friends and early in the war the house always seemed to be full of people. As time went by, many of the guests, some of whom were in the various regiments connected to the Brigadier, went off to battle. News of their whereabouts always seemed to find its way to 'Hammie', as the close friends of the Brigadier addressed him. As the war wore on and the young children went to school and the older children to war-work or jobs in the village, news would frequently arrive that was upsetting to the adults and even to us children.

One man who visited Hatch in 1940 was a commander in the Royal Canadian Navy named Charles T. Beard, a very brave man, who had commanded the HMCS Prince Robert in early 1940. He was an older man and was so nice to all the children. After a brief stay he left Hatch. In the following May of 1941, Mrs Shuckburgh came into the scullery where we were preparing the evening meal. She shook her head and kept saying, "How terrible, how terrible." I always liked Mrs Shuckburgh, and I asked her, "Madam, is something wrong?" She said, "Oh Eileen, you remember Commander Beard who was here some months ago?" And I said, "Yes." He had reminded me of the typical Naval Sea Dog from books I had read. She said, "We have just heard his only son, Thomas, was lost on the H.M.S. Hood in a fight against the (German pocket Battleship) Bismarck." He was a personal friend of the Gaunt family and I remembered him speaking kindly and lovingly of his son. Again, the war had brought a tragedy to all of us, even those to whom I had simply served dinner; a kind Naval Officer.

From the moment the war in France, in early June 1940, ended and the British stood alone, the reality of what the defeat in France meant to the British people and the soldiers of the BEF (British Expeditionary Force) began to spread to all parts of the country. The 'Miracle of Dunkirk,' as it has become to known over the years, saved the British Army, the British people and perhaps the Empire. It bought valuable time to re-group, re-equip, re-train, and re-arm the soldiers who had returned from the evacuation of the beaches of France. Although a crushing defeat, the Army had indeed survived to fight another day. The failure to destroy the BEF on the beaches was one of Hitler's great strategic military blunders. My mother had heard, as all of Britain had heard, of the titanic struggle going on in late May and early June in 1940 across the English Channel. What she didn't know was that she would come face to face with soldiers of France, Britain, Belgium and other countries in the village of Hatch.

We had ridden into the village in what the children called the dog cart (it was really a carriage pulled by a pony). The Brigadier loved to take a few children round the village in the cart to either pick up something from a village store or visit one of the local farmers and for us it was a chance to get out of the house and enjoy the fun of being with the Brigadier.

One afternoon in early June 1940, we had just started out on a local road and were all ready for an afternoon of excitement. I say 'excitement' because riding with him was nothing less than an experience; he was known to drive very fast around the country roads. He used to scare me to death. I know my sister Marie was with us (she always went anywhere she could with the Brigadier for she truly adored him) and one of the little boys who was staying at the house.

I noticed a number of ambulances speeding through Hatch, rounding the corners and heading for Taunton. Also, there were soldiers everywhere on the roads, walking slowly, some had obviously been wounded or had some type of injury. We all stared at them as they moved to the side of the road to let our cart pass. I saw men in uniforms I did not recognize. They for the most part just stared down at the road and rather than walk they shuffled or even staggered. We all became very quiet as we looked at these strangers. The ambulances kept coming, horns blaring with men inside the vehicles yelling, "Out of the way, make room, come on now move." Marie asked the Brigadier who these sad groups of soldiers were and where they had come from, as they looked so helpless and lost. He continued to sit in the cart for what seemed like a long time, just watching the men pass by, before he placed his hand on Marie's shoulder and said, "Marie, they have come from the coast, they are the soldiers who were rescued and have arrived from France."

We did not know where Dunkirk was, but had heard the men of the village talk about how badly the fight was going in France. I had seen some soldiers during our first months in Hatch, mostly Canadians who had arrived to help in the fight. What I did not know or understand at the time is that I was looking at men who had experienced defeat. They had blank stares and, although quiet, were grateful for the food and mugs of tea which the people watching handed them as they passed by. We could all tell the Brigadier was upset by what he was looking at; he had seen it before in the First World War and knew what these men had suffered, not just physically but mentally.

The ambulances passed through the village for days on end, as they made their way up from the coastal ports. You got used to them after awhile, but the sight of the poor men sitting on the side of the village roads to rest, was something neither I nor other children fully understood. We knew the war was not going well. The Brigadier spent most days in his study, the phone rang constantly and Canadian officers including Generals seemed to be coming with increasing frequency. Between trips to Aldershot, where he went frequently, or to surrounding billets, we saw little of the Brigadier during this time.

Things also began to change for the children. As servants started to leave for war, we were beginning to find we had to fend for ourselves more and more. The other older girls and I knew our life, full of new and exciting events, which had kept our initial time in Hatch so busy, was becoming more serious.

But, with all that was happening and changing in our little world, I (and I was by no means the only one) felt sorry for these young men, who were not much older than me and had already seen so much and experienced terrible things on the battlefields. As the men came through some would say, "Don't worry we will go back and get Adolf." Some smiled and said, "Hello", but for the most part they remained silent. I did not know these soldiers and many of them passed through the village unnoticed and forever unknown to us. Mrs Gault gave us sweets and said, "Take them down to the road and give them to the soldiers." We always did, but the looks on their faces was something you never forgot. Even children feel sorry for people they don't know, because we knew, even as young children, that their war was far from over.

I liked to think those men and the other soldiers who came to the house, all made it through the war, but I now know, many went to North Africa, as well as Europe and took part in D-Day and never returned.

In 1940 and 1941, a few of the Canadian soldiers became well known around Hatch Court and both Mrs Gault and the

Brigadier developed a true fondness for them. Three of them were Captain George Corkett, Lt. Bob Osler, and a handsome young Lieutenant of the Princess Patricia's who I knew only as Rusty. They were stationed in the surrounding areas for training and, as members of the Brigadier's famous regiment, were always welcome at the house. Actually, Hatch Court was in some ways a home away from home for any soldier, particularly a member of the Pat's.

Lt. Bob Osler, who was a Patricia and was attached to the 48th Highlanders of Canada, was killed in Sicily in August 1943. 'Rusty' would ask if he could help me, when I was working in the house. Actually, he sometimes followed me around, I think trying to find a reason to offer his help. He once asked me to a dance, but, at 16, I did not have the courage to ask Mrs Gault if I could go to a dance with a young officer. She had refused my dance requests so many times that I had become a bit sheepish about bringing the subject up! When this wonderful young man, who was so full of life, was killed in Italy, I felt I had lost a friend. As the war progressed I was learning, as were millions of people, what true sadness felt like.

When I first saw Captain Corkett in 1940 and later when Lieutenant Osler came in 1941, I was 13 and 14 years of age. To say I thought they were handsome and dashing in their uniforms would be quite an understatement. I developed a crush on Captain Corkett the first minute I saw him. He was so kind to us, so handsome at the age of 24 and very much in love with a beautiful young lady of just 19 years of age, named Aileen Townsend. They spent Easter 1940 at Hatch and were soon married. They made a couple that could have been in any wartime movie love story. They were perfect for each other and you could see that they were very much in love.

I remember thinking to myself; someday I would like to fall in love with someone like that. My time was a few years away, but in 1940 I could not have known that. During the next few years Captain George R. Corkett fought bravely in Sicily, suffered a wound to his head and become an acting Major in the Coldstream Guards. He visited Hatch numerous times, danced with my sister Marie, (the first dance she ever had), and was awarded the Africa Star in January 1944 for his bravery and leadership under fire. He played games in the grounds with all the evacuees. After recovering from his wounds with his devoted Aileen at his side, he returned to the fighting and then on September 22nd 1944, at the age of 28, he was killed in battle in Italy.

The unthinkable had happened to one of the most popular officers to come to Hatch Court. Mrs Gault called those of us who were there that day into the long room, her voice breaking, she said, "Our wonderful Captain Corkett has been lost in Italy." I cannot ever remember a sadder day ever at Hatch Court. Everyone was so fond of him and his wife, who by then was expecting their first child. He was a brave man, a wonderfully kind person to everyone. He also had a wonderful singing voice.

Mrs Gault always wanted him to sit behind her when we went to church so she could hear him sing and then he was killed at such a young age. The Brigadier, Mrs Gault, Mrs Shuckburgh, the servants and all of the evacuees were truly affected by his loss. I had seen Mrs Gault become emotional before as the news brought to the Court was often not pleasant. Many friends of the Gaults were lost as the war dragged on, but nothing I can remember, cast such despair over everyone as the death of this wonderful young man.

The sadness has always remained with me, because this soldier and his wife had become part of Hatch Court. He was more than a face passing on a village road. The death of this young man brought me to tears and made me understand how terrible the events around us truly were. We never saw Aileen again. She returned to Canada and shortly thereafter gave birth to their daughter, Georgeanne.

In the early 1970s, after returning to Hatch Court to visit my sister and Mrs Gault, who was coming to the end of her long life, I was surprised to find that Aileen Howes (née Corkett) was well and still living in Canada. Marie was even able to give me her address and so began a 25 year exchange of letters. She had remarried and rebuilt her life and, from her letters, seemed the same warm person I had known at Hatch during the war. She had also remained friends with Captain (later Major General) C.B. Ware, a former commanding officer of George Corkett in the Princess Patricia's. My son, Mike, began a correspondence with General Ware about the General's

WWII experiences and a friendship developed between them until General Ware's death in 1995.

In November 1945, Marie and I went to the Remembrance Service at the Cenotaph in London. It was very sad, but in a way, wonderful. We went into Westminster Abbey and in the churchyard was a beautiful Garden of Remembrance. We put three little crosses in Canada's Garden, for Captain Corkett, Lt. Osler and Rusty and on the note, we wrote, "From the evacuees at Hatch Court." How strange it was, that during the two minutes silence, I thought of Captain Corkett and remembered him singing a song called 'Blue Skies' whilst he polished his boots by the clock tower at Hatch.

Even today, Captain Corkett has not been forgotten; high in the mountains of Manitoba, the Canadian government honoured him by naming a lake in his memory, Corkett Lake. It seems very fitting that his name has not been lost to history and particularly touching, for Aileen, his widow, and those who, like my mother, had met him.

Although the loss of these people; brave soldiers, fellow evacuees and others who had passed through our young lives were truly sad events, nothing could compare with the sadness caused by the loss of my mum. That broke the hearts of my sister, brothers and me and the memory still brings tears to my eyes to this day. We were told of her death in May 1941, but it was not until we returned to London after the war, that we found out that my mum had actually died three months earlier, in February. My poor father could not bear to tell us such sad news with us so far away from home. I cannot, even now, explain why my father never told us where my mum was buried. Perhaps worse than his grief and whatever reasons he had, was my own stupidity in not insisting that we were told, so we could visit her to say our final goodbyes.

I was to leave England in 1946 and go to America. My father passed away in 1948 and with his death took the whereabouts of my mum's grave with him. Even now, I do not know where she is buried, nor did my sister and brothers ever find out. What a true sadness not to know where my mother's grave is.

Chapter 11

The Yanks- 1942

At about this time, rumours had started about the U.S. Army coming to the village, but we didn't pay much attention because rumours were flying everywhere. The U.S. Forces had been pouring into England and everyone thought, "Who are those unruly, brash, ill-mannered people who play dice on street corners, ride their bikes on the footpaths with radios blaring, whistling at the girls and grabbing them as they walk by." There were thousands stationed in the West Country, but millions all over Britain. It is still unbelievable to think how that little country, smaller than the state of Texas, could have absorbed all those men from all over the world with all their equipment, materials and blend them into the towns, villages and countryside.

There was great excitement in our little village of Hatch Beauchamp. Hatch Park was being prepared for a company of U.S. soldiers. An Army camp was being built, by black U.S. troops, in the ruins of the Park, which sat in the middle of the village. They came every day, but we never saw them, because they came early in the mornings and left at night.

In Hatch Beauchamp, in addition to Hatch Court, there was another large manor house across the road, up a similar long, winding, tree-lined drive. I remember that, although not as large as Hatch Court, it was, nonetheless, a beautiful estate. Hatch Park had been built years after 'The Court', but was the only other house that had as much farmland and it would serve as home to the American army units that would arrive in late 1942. Whenever I walked through the village, I always looked past the gate, up the road leading to the 'other' large house. Little did I know in 1939, when we first arrived there from London, how important Hatch Park would become in my life just a few years later.

The house at Hatch Park belonged to Commander and Lady Alice Gore-Langton. She was a direct descendant of Queen Victoria and really was the 'Lady' of the village, although Mrs Gault, never one to be outdone, would not readily have accepted that!

> *Hatch Park had 12 evacuees from North London and one terrible night, a fire destroyed the house. The poor children had to jump out of the windows and many were hurt. Miss Tennant, the nanny of the Gore-Langton children, went back into the house to make sure all the children had escaped and she was burnt to death. The evacuee children from Hatch Park were then billeted throughout the village. It was such a great tragedy to have this loss of life. The house was never rebuilt and none of us ever knew where Commander and Mrs Gore-Langton went to live.*

When I visited Hatch Beauchamp in 2010, I was able to discover what had happened to the owners, the evacuees who were housed there and the house itself. Thanks to John Townsend and his friend, Clare Jordan (née Gore-Langton), the granddaughter of Commander Alearic Gore-Langton, I learned that after the fire in 1940, the house lay in ruins throughout the rest of the war. The children were moved to other village homes, who could take them, in the area, though not all remained in Hatch Beauchamp.

Commander and Lady Gore-Langton moved into a smaller house on his estate known as 'The Lodge.' Village lore has it that a vast amount of silver and other valuables were stored in the basement of the house prior to the fire, to protect it in case the house was destroyed by German bombing, or perhaps in case of a German invasion, and could still be there today. To date, no-one has discovered if this is the case!

As I walked slowly around the grounds of Hatch Park, I could see where the old house had once stood (I still have a picture of my father taken in 1943 standing by the ruins of the burned house). I wondered if, beneath the mound of dirt and debris that lay to the left of the rebuilt house, there was still a treasure trove of valuables that has lain untouched since that terrible day that the house burned down, claiming the life of the caring Miss Tennant.

Miss Tennant is buried in the village churchyard, alongside my Aunt Marie and other villagers who played a part in my mother's life during the war years.

By the middle of 1942, Britain was subject to an invasion, a friendly invasion, but an invasion nonetheless. The United States Army and Air Corps began coming to the British Isles. At first it was a trickle of soldiers, but that quickly turned into a flood of young, handsome, eager and, in many cases, very naïve young men. Their motto seemed to be, "Where the hell is this god-damned war? Let's get it over with."

Little did any of them know what the next three years would bring. Hundreds of thousands would never return from the countless battles that were to come and would spend forever in resting places throughout Europe. Many are buried in England, in immaculate cemeteries that are the silent reminders of their bravery and sacrifice.

In early 1942, however, those battles were ahead of them and the order of the day was to adjust to being away from home, prepare for battle and to learn to get along with the British people. In many cases, the latter would prove a very tough assignment.

As the Americans landed in parts of Scotland, Ireland, and England, they encountered everything from warm welcomes, resistance, indifference and, in some cases, outright hostility. It wasn't so much that the British disliked Americans, although some did. (Perhaps they still hadn't forgotten the little incident with the colonies in 1776). But, to say the least, the Americans were different.

My mother described her first experience of seeing and meeting American soldiers in the village of Hatch as one of the most unforgettable experiences in her young life:

I had been to school and was walking home with the other village children on a beautiful autumn day in October 1942. The days were warm and the nights had just started to turn cool after sunset. Hatch Beauchamp looked like a picture post card and even though the war continued all around us, so did village life.

You have to remember that very little motor traffic and trucks passed through the village, as petrol rationing left few people with the luxury of being able to drive their cars. In fact, there were not many cars in the village to begin with. Apart from the Brigadier's beautiful Bentley and Rolls Royce, there were only 6 other people who had cars. A few others had trucks, but many used farm wagons and some even rode horses and it was still exciting to see one of the locals gallop through the village. We were used to trucks and the smell of their diesel, but for kids from the East End, horses were a treat and great fun to see.

So as we trooped back to The Court from school, a rumbling, ear-splitting noise grew from down Curry Mallet Road. It was army trucks starting to pour through the village. I had seen British army trucks before. The first time was when streams of trucks and ambulances brought back our troops from the coast after Dunkirk a few years earlier. But these were different, not only were the trucks models we had never seen, they were a dull green and covered with big white stars. All of us jumped back from the road and stood by the bushes that lined Curry Mallet Road and stared wide-eyed as this seemingly endless line of green vehicles roared past us throwing up giant clouds of dust. There had been all sorts of rumours going around as to what these crazy Yanks were doing and we locals were scared to death of them.

We had also heard there were Americans in a few of the surrounding villages and Mrs Gault said she had seen some American Officers in Taunton a few weeks before. Now they were in front of our very eyes. It was then that the first truck went by us and standing in the back waving, as though they were leaving the dock on an Ocean liner for a vacation, were American G.I.s. They were not only waving, but yelling like Red Indians from the Wild West movies we had seen in the picture house; "Hey Blondie, how about a date?", "Hey sweetie, where's the nearest Pub?" And for my brothers and the other little village boys, out of the back of the trucks came flying packs of gum, Hershey Chocolate bars, and even a few packs of American cigarettes. Although the trucks never stopped, the G.I.s continued to wave and yell the same things. A few of their comments cannot be printed here but they were amazing to hear.

They had not yet been in battle and many of them had never been away from home before, so to them it must have seemed like a holiday. That would change quickly. But for that day, for that moment, seeing the Americans for the first time was both exciting and memorable. I know I will never forget it.

For my mother and others in the village of Hatch that day, the sight of those first few trucks bringing the first Americans would soon become a regular occurrence, with a flood of Americans arriving over the next few months. It was hard for the villagers to understand that these men, who certainly looked the part of the great American Army, were just from small towns in America having had very little education and here they were coming to Britain to prepare for the invasion of the European continent. These young Americans were, however, to make a few stops before reaching Hatch Park.

In early October 1943, my father's troopship (which was the famous Ocean liner Mauretania) docked in Liverpool, England. Along with 12,000 other soldiers, my dad disembarked and started a three year journey which was to change his life and bring my mother and father together, for what was to be a lifetime of shared memories. My father's unit was attached to the First Army, 28th Division. Later in the war, after he arrived in France, his outfit would be attached to the Third Army commanded by the illustrious, if somewhat controversial, General George Patton.

After their arrival in England the troops were moved to various camps throughout the country. My father's unit was transferred to the area near Taunton, not far from Hatch Beauchamp. Their first stop on arrival in Somerset was at the small village of Ilminster. His outfit set up their first camp in Dillington Park, in the grounds of Dillington House.

The history of Dillington House can readily be traced back to 1551. In the beginning of the 17th century it is believed the house itself was extended to occupy its present site and its current E shape plan and layout. The house was remodelled in 1838. The remodelling was under the direction of Sir James Pennethorne. Pennethorne did much of the 19th century construction of what are now considered some of England's most famous landmarks; buildings such as the western buildings of Somerset House and the ballroom of Buckingham Palace. He also laid out St James Park, Victoria Park, Battersea Park and Kensington Gardens. The present day interior of the house still combines a sense of dignity and intimacy.

During the Second World War, Dillington was commandeered by the Government to help with the war effort. From October 1939 until March 1940, Dillington was the temporary headquarters of the RASC 507th territorial Company. When the war intensified, as part of the 44th Home Counties Division, they moved out of the grounds to another part of Somerset. It was then Dillington saw elements of the American Army arrive. The grounds around Dillington became a sea of tents that were later replaced with Nissen Huts. To the east of the main house a large vehicle assembly area was set up.

After the first contingent of American troops arrived, a black construction battalion expanded the vehicle area and living facilities. They became popular with the local villagers for their friendliness and professionalism. They then moved on and were replaced by American combat troops. Additionally, a U.S. Corps headquarters was established in the nearby town of Taunton (*Dillington House History was taken from "The story of Dillington House - A Thousand Year History, by Nancy Smith*).

It was to this picturesque, but busy location, that elements of my father's division established their regimental headquarters in October 1943, shortly after their arrival from the United States. A postcard from my father and a picture of him standing in front of Dillington house was found in his belongings after his death, and shows Dillington House as it was when he first arrived.

Remarkably, the house has changed little in appearance in the past 67 years. I remember my father's description of his first impression of this imposing house that was to be their headquarters. He said they arrived on a typical English late autumn morning after an all night move from the coastal areas. As the morning mist lifted from the low lying fields the form of this magnificent house took shape.

The convoy stopped and, as the tents, huts and massed array of vehicles began to come into focus, many of his fellow soldiers stood in silence as the main house and grounds loomed before them. He mentioned he lit a cigarette turned to his corporal and said, "That is the biggest house I have ever seen." The corporals response was a simple, "Sarge, that is the biggest anything I have ever seen."

The tents and vehicles were spread out around the grounds and where possible under the protection of trees. This was to keep the prying eyes of a stray German fighter or bomber from seeing what would become part of the men and vehicle build up to D-Day still eight months away. His unit only remained at Dillington for a short time before they were moved to Hatch Beauchamp, but he always remembered his first view of the large English estate and house. Dillington continued to remain a requisitioned property for the U.S. Army during the build up to D-Day, and afterwards officers of the U.S. Army Air Corps and elements of the famed 101st division are believed to have made use of the House and its grounds until late 1944.

While visiting Somerset in 2010, I asked to be taken to Dillington House. John Townsend drove me to the magnificent, stately home on a perfect spring day in April. As we talked about the surrounding countryside and the beauty of England in the spring, we came upon a picture postcard house (if a mansion can be classified as a house). We were not far from Hatch Beauchamp, less than 8 miles, and I felt drawn to visit the area where my father was billeted so many years ago when he first arrived in England.

As we made our way up the long tree - lined drive, I looked over the fields and hills surrounding the Dillington House Estate. I tried to picture what these fields looked like in 1943. Today little if anything is left of the American presence, just a concrete road that leads to nowhere, and a stray line of fence that to the casual eye looks out of place in these grounds that are so green and beautiful. But if you look very closely you can still see signs of the war and of the Americans, they are faded true, but they are there nonetheless.

As more and more American soldiers and vehicles arrived in 1943, they soon outgrew the area and moved on to Hatch Park in Hatch Beauchamp about eight miles away. This was to be their home until the invasion in 1944.

As they built their camps in Hatch Park and other local villages, the Americans had a difficult time adjusting to England, whose people were used to the hardships and devastation of war. As many a G.I. would remember; England was always cold, the beer always warm and the people were always seemingly indifferent. In Hatch Beauchamp they met people who were used to the cold, loved warm beer and were for the most part indifferent. But there were the exceptions; the village children and the village teenage girls. My mother recalls meeting one of those Americans just a few days after their arrival.

One very cold afternoon, I rode my bike to the Post Office to deliver the post. As I propped it up against the wall, a jeep full of GIs stopped just in front of me. I was scared to death. This handsome Sergeant said to me, "Your hands are cold, here take my gloves." I stood up straight and looked him directly in the eye and politely said, "Thanks, but no thanks." I wouldn't have dreamed of taking anything from him even if I was freezing to death. Little did I know then how much time would be spent with this handsome young Sergeant in the future.

Robert M. Burns – 1942

Sgt. Robert M. Burns - Marseille, France

Robert Burns at entrance to Hatch Park

St John's Church behind Hatch Court

Chapter 12

Romance Blossoms

As everyone settled into the Village, there were weekly dances at the local Village Hall. Some of the American GIs brought their own music from the U.S. Most of it we had not heard, nor had we ever seen most of the dances they were doing. The Jitterbug - what was that? Oh, it looked like so much fun I was determined to learn it.

One Saturday night, Rosemary and I went to the dance which was full of GIs. We were standing at the back of the room looking around at the GIs. I leaned over to Rosemary and said, "Who do you like the look of?" She said, "See that Sgt standing there?" I said, "You mean the one standing in the middle of the group?" She said, "Yes." I said, "Hands off, he's mine." She said, "Oh Eileen, you don't even know him!" I said, "No, but I will before the night is over."

When the evening began, we did what we always did which was to sit on the chairs and just wait for someone to ask us to dance. I looked up and there was that handsome Sgt walking towards me. As he walked the length of the room I started to shake. I was so hoping he was really going to ask me to dance. He stopped just in front of me and said, "Hey, let's dance." I sat there for just a second looking at him. I couldn't believe his nerve to just approach me and say, "Hey, let's dance." You see, I was used to having English boys approach me and say, "May I have this dance?" They would ask you, not tell you. But here was this handsome GI before me and I really wanted to learn how to jitterbug. I thought "What the hell." As we approached the dance floor I was hoping he couldn't tell I had butterflies in my stomach, but the nerves quickly slipped away as we began to dance. Oh, what a wonderful dancer he was. I felt like I was floating on a cloud.

One of the first things I noticed about him was how immaculately dressed he was, with his perfectly starched uniform and how heavenly he smelled. He introduced himself, his name was Sergeant Robert 'Bob' Burns and he was from Steubenville, Ohio. As we danced and began to talk, we *realized that it was him that offered me the gloves at the Post Office and we had quite a laugh. What a chance meeting this turned out to be, not once but twice. More than anything else that evening, not only was I with a handsome young man, I was learning the jitterbug!*

As the months went by, Bob and I started to see quite a lot of each other when the opportunities arose. We would continue to meet at the Village Hall for dances and just had wonderful times.

The Village Hall was a place where Glenn Miller's and Tommy Dorsey's music was played, and the young girls and soldiers danced the jitterbug and escaped from the war that surrounded all of them.

The American troops from nearby Hatch Park and sometimes British soldiers, whose billets were in other camps in the area, also came to the dance with the local girls from the surrounding villages. With the Americans now located in the village and British troops, who had returned from Dunkirk and fought in North Africa and Sicily, relations with what the British considered the 'untested' Americans, was not always the warmest.

The English troops were not paid or equipped nearly as well as the average GI and did not care for how the 'Yanks' would sweep the girls off their feet. My father recalled a dance at the local village hall when British soldiers came in during the evening. Immediately tensions rose between the allies and at some time during the evening the coat sleeves of the GIs jackets that were hanging in the cloak room were slashed by British soldiers. While very upset and words were exchanged, most of the Americans realized it was a sense of frustration from the British men, not necessarily hatred towards the Americans. Captain Burns (my dad's Commanding Officer) told Brigadier Gault of the incident. The Brigadier got the British Commanding Officer to line up the soldiers who were at the dance for questioning, no-one ever admitted to it. Nonetheless, my father never hung his coat up in a cloakroom at any more of the dances.

I knew Bob had other girlfriends around the villages. I didn't blame him as a lot of village girls were swept off their feet by the Americans. All the girls hung around him but I never did. I don't think he could understand that. We were just good friends and enjoyed each other's company and whenever we were together, he always treated me like a lady. He always knew where he stood with me and only once in awhile did he try to act like the GIs one would hear about. He was soon told off and put in his place.

One beautiful Sunday afternoon we had taken a long walk to Crimson Hill. When we were getting ready to head back, Bob said, "It is a long way back I don't know if I can make it." I said, "I know a short cut, here through the woods." As we walked slowly back, we stopped in a clearing underneath a tree, sat and just talked. A few minutes later, I felt this hand on my left thigh, high up the thigh at that. I said, "What are you doing?" He said, "What? What do you mean?" I said, "Move your hand!" His response was, "But I don't have any place to put my hand." I jumped up and said, "Have you ever thought of putting it in your pocket?" I was horrified and stood away from him and said, "Don't you ever do that again!" He apologized and said he would never do that again. And he didn't.

He did, however, once more push his luck; one day while we were out taking a walk, he asked me if I would wash his clothes. I looked at him appalled. The absolute nerve of that man! So the next day I sent him a box of Oxydol all wrapped up in brown paper with a note, "This is so you can do your own washing." Charles and Dennis went to the camp and gave it to the guard to give to Sgt Burns. Bob couldn't believe that I would send a box of washing powder to him, but I think I made my point.

He used to tell me he could bring all kinds of things from the PX. He said, "All the other GIs were bringing things for their girlfriends." I said, "No Bob, I don't want to be obligated to you." I know he probably thought I was nuts for refusing much needed necessities, but that's the way I was. I didn't really know him well enough to accept gifts and never wanted to hear, "But I gave you all those things", and that is the way I wanted to keep it. That was the first time I felt he considered me a 'girlfriend'. Nonetheless, I was not going to accept any gifts.

By our second official date, I knew I was in love with him. Mrs Gault, of course, went out of her mind at the very thought of me dating a GI. She told me all kinds of things *that, naturally, I just ignored. She was through running my life. I was old enough to make my own decisions.*

The camp had a dance and the Brigadier and Mrs Gault were invited. The Brigadier, being aware that I was friendly with a GI, knew that I wanted to go. He said, "Oh, there's no room in the car, I fear you will have to hold on and ride on the running board." I had already served dinner in my beautiful red dress, so I put on my silver shoes, put a red velvet bow in my hair, which I stole out of the 'Bundles for Britain' sacks and off we went, riding on the running board and holding on for dear life. As we pulled into the camp, a lot of the GIs had just showered and were standing half naked in their tents. They shouted and whistled and whooped until someone said, "Hey, that's Sgt Burns' girl." Then all became much quieter. We walked into the mess hall and there were big beef sandwiches, kegs of beer and a wonderful band and, of course, there was Sgt Burns. We had such a wonderful time. We jitterbugged and danced up a storm. Mrs Gault leaned over to me and said, "Eileen, where on earth did you learn those dances?" I just smiled at her. The Gaults left and the dance continued until midnight. Bob and I stood in the village and talked for a long time. He walked me home as he usually did, but neither of us spoke. I had so many thoughts running through my mind. I think Bob too was thinking about our friendship and what the future held for us. When he walked me home, it was always only part of the way. I could never understand why.

Apparently when my father was stationed in nearby Hatch Park and began dating my mother he always walked her to the back entrance of Hatch, and due to the blackout conditions in effect throughout England at that time, he always carried a flashlight or 'torch' as the British called them. After he said goodnight to my mother, he would, in his words "run like hell back to camp", in the pitch dark until he reached the guard at the gate of his camp. I often kidded him about being a fearless American soldier.

That was until I went to Hatch Court in 1985 for the first time. My girlfriend, who became my wife of 22 years, my Aunt, and I, left Hatch one evening to return to the cottage we had rented for our stay in the village. We left the Court after a wonderful evening of conversation with Commander and Mrs Barry Nation, Anne, the Commander's wife, being Mrs Hamilton Gault's niece. As we walked back to the cottage in the pitch dark, I was reminded of my father's tale, and found myself leaving my Aunt and future wife in the shadows and 'running like hell' back to the cottage, just as the American Sergeant had done many years before. Fear of darkness and shadows must still run in our family.

I relate this story because I can only imagine what must have gone through my mother's mind those nights, when she would leave a dance, a friend's house, or the old Hatch Inn, and walk through the blackness up a long path to 'The Court' with only the reflection from the moon to guide her. For the evacuees, as for all British people in those days, getting around in the dark was something they just got used to.

Spring went into summer and we dated steadily. One Sunday, we were standing outside the Hatch Inn which was a pub, restaurant and hotel when he asked me to come inside with him. I said, "No, I don't go into the Inn." He opened the door and there was a lovely sitting room, so I went inside. I was scared to death that someone would see me there. He proceeded to read a letter from a girl named Mabel. She was a girl he had been dating for about 2 years in Steubenville, Ohio and he said he intended to marry her when he went back home. I felt the walls come crashing around me and with a lump in my throat I simply wished him the best and told him I hoped they would be happy. However, we continued to date and Mabel was never mentioned again.

Then one night, as he walked me home from a dance, he kissed me. He had kissed me before but this was different. I knew then that I really was in love with him. So I said, "Bob, I love you." He looked at me and said, "Please don't say that, don't." I simply looked at him and said, "Well, I'm sorry but I do."

After that night, for some reason, we just stopped dating. It must have been what I said to him. I didn't see him for weeks. I had the feeling that he knew our relationship was turning into a love affair and wasn't sure what to do, so he had decided to keep his distance from me. After all, he was still engaged to Mabel in the States. Even though I had hoped things would turn out to be different, I knew they were not going to. I was heartbroken, but I just had to carry on.

I continued to go to the dances. Then one Saturday night, I put on my red velvet dress and silver shoes and went to the dance upstairs at the Hatch Inn. I walked in amid whistles and comments from all the GIs. There, as large as life, was Bob surrounded by half the village girls including Rosemary Spain. I, of course, completely ignored him and sat down across the room from them. I was never short of a dancing partner and was having a great time even though my heart was across the room. A Ladies' Choice was announced, so I went up to Bob and asked him to dance. Rosemary quickly leapt in saying, "I have already asked him." I said, "Oh, I am terribly sorry", excused myself and walked back across the room. Just before I sat down, a GI caught my arm and said, "You're not sitting down", and we danced.

A few minutes later Bob came across to me and said, "Let's dance." I walked out onto the dance floor and he just continued to walk right passed me back to his little group without saying a word. I wasn't going to let that just pass! The next Ladies' Choice I made sure the dance floor was empty and asked him to dance. I followed him onto the dance floor, and looked him in the eye as I continued to walk past him and said, "Nobody leaves me on the dance floor alone." He was left standing on the dance floor alone, his ego crushed I am sure, but I didn't care.

I passed Mrs Fowler, who was a WVS Lady and she said, "Eileen, Sgt Burns is in love with you." I said, "Well, it doesn't look like it", as I watched Bob push Rosemary around the dance floor. I looked at this GI who was standing next to me and I said, "Let's dance up a storm." We jitterbugged and laughed (I was really playing for attention) and I noticed out of the corner of my eye, Bob was watching me and not very happy that I was having such a good time. So be it. I walked home that night alone and was so very sad that Sgt Burns was not walking with me.

The next weekend, as I was not seeing Bob anymore, I began dating a GI in Taunton and went to a picture show. When I got off the bus at the Hatch Inn, I heard a voice calling my name. I looked around and there was Sgt Burns leaning out of the window at the Club. He said, "Come on up." I said, "If you want to speak to me, you come down here." I really didn't expect him to, but down he came. We started talking at the front gate and he said, "Let's go up and sit down." So we went upstairs to sit down and started talking.

He said "Eileen, I have really missed you." I just laughed and said, "How could you possibly miss me when I hear you have been having a high old time with Rosemary Spain and Beattie Vile? Vile by name and vile by nature." He roared with laughter and said, "You certainly know how to put in the knife and give it a twist", and with that he said, "I have a date with Rosemary tonight."

I was looking out of the window and saw her come flying into the yard on her bicycle. I said, "Lucky you and here she comes." Rosemary came running up the stairs and almost dropped dead in the doorway. Bob had his back to the door and I was looking straight at her. She stood stock still, then walked in and past us and said, "Hello Bob, Hello Eileen." We just went on talking and she stood at the end of the hall. I said to Bob, "Aren't you going to say something to your girlfriend?" He said, "She's not my girlfriend."

Bob and I continued to talk and as we turned to leave Rosemary was nowhere in sight. She obviously realized she had no date for the night. We left and walked up Curry Mallet Road. He jumped up in the hedge and said, "Give me your hand and I'll help you up." I said, "I don't get up in hedges with American Soldiers." He laughed and said, "But I'm Bob." I said, "All the more reason that I'm not getting up there." We continued on our walk and it began to rain.

In some parts of England, even today, there are places where time seems to have stood still. In many ways Hatch Beauchamp is one of those places. In the crisp April days when I returned to Hatch in 2010, I saw the Hatch Inn on the corner where it has stood for over a hundred years. My parents said during the war it was one of the most popular 'haunts' of American, British, and Canadian soldiers who passed through the village. But, more importantly to me, it was where my mother and father spent their evenings at dances and just sitting and talking about their lives, the war, and the future.

Up the road is the old village school where my mother and her family went to lessons and where today local children are still taught. As I was standing in front of the school, something caught my eye, an old red telephone box, (the kind that used to be on virtually every corner in the country) with paint peeling, phone removed and cracked glass. A relic left from another time, but this particular telephone box had been a part of my parent's life at Hatch during the war, and part of the story they had both related on my first visit to the village in 1985.

I had known all along that we were not just dating one another, but I kept hearing rumours that Bob was certainly dating his fair share of local village girls in Curry Mallet, Isle Abbots, Curry Rivel, Ilminster and even in the town of Taunton. I was determined not to be just one of his many girlfriends in one of the villages. Either Bob and I were going to have an understanding, or Sergeant Burns would have to find himself another girl, for it seemed I was more serious about our relationship than he was. After all, I had already told him that I loved him and I didn't really know how he felt. It was time for us to talk!

With rain lightly falling, we continued our walk to nowhere. I became very quiet with all kinds of thoughts running through my mind. Bob had asked me a number of times if something was wrong. I had repeatedly lied and said, "No, everything is fine." Finally as he tried his level best to make conversation I finally said to him, "So how is Violet in Curry Rivel?" He looked shocked and said, "What do you mean?" I told him I had heard he was seeing other girls from surrounding villages and I thought that perhaps we should end our friendship. He started to mumble about he had just danced with other girls like I danced with other GIs. I thought that's it and said, "I must return to The Court." With that I turned to go back. He said, "Wait Eileen, let me explain", and followed me.

We found our way back to the Hatch Inn. It was as always, pitch black and the lane beside the Inn was nearly deserted. He walked quickly to my side and from the light of his torch (GI flashlight) he pointed to the nearby telephone box and said, "Let's step in here out of the rain and talk for a moment." I thought to myself "As if I am going to squash into a phone box and listen to some worn out excuse." After a few moments of listening to him and standing there in the rain, I reluctantly agreed to step into the phone box and hear him out. I looked down the lane and back to the dimly lit door of the Inn and said, "All right then, I will listen to you, but only for a moment, I do not want to be seen in a phone box with some American GI."

He went into some long rather dubious excuse of his village travels with his fellow soldiers and pledged that neither Violet nor anyone else meant anything to him; they *were just someone to dance with when I wasn't around. He then leaned forward to kiss me. I quickly pulled away, thanked him for his explanation and said, "Good night Sergeant." With that I ran through the darkness and up the side path to the house. I was, of course, rather pleased with myself. I had made Bob explain his actions and extracted a pledge of what I felt was a commitment that our relationship had taken a step towards becoming more serious and that was all right in my mind. It was what I had hoped would happen. He never would know how deeply in love I felt that night, at least not for a few more years.*

As I stood staring at the old phone booth, I thought of that story and how so many years ago the young, pretty evacuee thought she had outsmarted the slightly overconfident and I am sure somewhat full of himself, American Sergeant. I walked backed to the car, shook my head, smiled to myself, and whispered, "Way to go, Mom."

As the buzz of an invasion continued to mount, my mother knew her sergeant would be going to France at some point, she just didn't know when. The invasion had been talked about for so many months and rumours were the order of the day. After all, my father's unit for months had been preparing equipment for the invasion and he seemed to my mother to have grown quieter and more withdrawn in the last week or so. She knew he would probably be leaving soon and her concern was his safety as well as their blossoming romance. She truly had fallen in love with her American and did not want to lose him or see him go.

One day whilst out on her bike, my mother saw some paratroopers in the village. She had seen the dashing 'paras' before as the British 'Red Devils' had passed through the Hatch area a few months earlier. She had asked the Brigadier who these fearsome looking Americans were. He said, "Brave men Eileen, who will soon be going to France." He then said quietly, so softly she could barely hear him, "Many of them will never come back." Brigadier Gault knew what was in store for the soldiers, as he had been witness to death on the battlefields of France only some 20 years before.

Not many miles from Taunton was a village called Upottery. For months it had been home to elements of the famous American 101st Airborne division. When my uncles were young they had spent months watching the paratroopers in the surrounding countryside as they were on manoeuvres. The soldiers never failed to give my uncles a bar of chocolate or a stick of gum, much sought after treats for the evacuees.

On the night of the 5th June, I was in bed when I heard aeroplanes overhead. Aeroplanes going on bombing missions were nothing new, but this sounded different. They began around 10.00pm and the roar of the engines seemed endless. The planes seemed to fill the sky and their engines drowned out all other noise. I crawled out on to the rooftop when I heard new sounds, as was my custom, even though it was forbidden. I looked into the night sky and saw an endless stream of planes overhead. I saw bombers, C-47 transporters, gliders being towed, fighter planes and other planes of size and description I had never seen. I knew then this was not an ordinary night, THIS MUST BE THE INVASION!

It was a late afternoon in June; my mother was excited as she had a date that evening with my father and it had been a week since she had last seen him. He told her he had been restricted to quarters until further notice. She wasn't sure what that meant or why, because what was important to her was my dad had sent a message to her that he would be able to get out of camp for a few hours on Thursday. My mother recalled that it had been a strange few weeks. School was disrupted by convoy and troop movements all around the area. There were also an unusually large number of visitors to Hatch, some of whom were high ranking officers and their ladies. Lt. Colonel Jimmie Gault had also been to the house recently for a weekend visit.

So while serving as parlour-maid, my mother was also kept busy with all the visitors and guests, setting tables and serving food. While not her lifelong dream, it was what she was paid to do and she received the royal wage of sixpence a week for her efforts. At the time, Hatch Court appeared to be the busiest place in England and to a sixteen year old girl from the East End, one of the most exciting places she could imagine. Two weeks before, D-Day had finally arrived, on June 6, 1944. The long awaited invasion of Europe had finally taken place.

In anticipation of my evening out with Bob, I went to the back gate at Hatch Park and waited for him. As I was standing in the twilight, an old gentleman was pushing his bike up the road that ran next to the American encampment. He nodded and said, "What are you waiting for dear?" I said rather proudly, "I have a date with a GI and we are to meet here." He stopped, looked at me and said, "They have all left, love, they headed for the coast just a little while ago." I could still hear the roar of trucks moving in the park and I thought something was happening. I stood there transfixed and just stared at the elderly man. I was so very sad at that moment. There was to be no goodbye, no last conversation, no outpouring of the heart or a final farewell kiss. The Americans, my American, had gone to France.

As I turned to go back to The Court, I felt the tears running down my cheeks. Not only were they tears for Bob, but for all the young men who had spent that last year at Hatch Beauchamp. When I got back, I went onto the roof and could hear men shouting orders. I still couldn't believe it, even though in the back of my mind I knew it was wartime and our time together would not last. What Bob did not know as he left, was he was taking my heart with him. It had been so wonderful while it lasted. I just wished I had said goodbye and told him that I loved him.

The soldiers who had been in Hatch Beauchamp during the last year had become part of the village life. Their humour, kindness and American ways of doing things had changed the village and many people in it forever. Would they ever come back? More importantly, would Eileen's Sergeant ever return or would she never hear from him again? There were no answers, just the emptiness and sadness that she had not felt since standing at the train station in September 1939 and waving goodbye to her parents. But life had to go on. She still had to take care of her brothers and sister and continue her job as the parlour-maid. War or no war, there was still much to do.

Time seemed to drag as I went about my daily duties. Almost every day, Mrs Shuckburgh would ask, "Eileen, have you heard from your American friend?" And sadly I would say, "No." I almost didn't expect to ever hear from him again, I just hoped. Three weeks went by and my sister Marie said, "Eileen, you have a letter from Bob." I broke into a run as though a bomb had fallen on top of Hatch Court. Marie said, "It's just a letter Eileen, don't break your neck. If you break your neck you won't be able to read the letter!" The letter was, indeed, from Bob, dated August 6th 1944. He was somewhere in France and had been very busy. He apologized for not being able to get in touch with me before he left, but mostly he complained of not being able to get any beer, only cider and wine and he asked that I write to him soon. Needless to say I was over the moon with excitement.

I dashed to my room and wrote the first of many letters. I wrote to him every day. After I received the first two letters from him, weeks went by and I didn't hear from him. I began to get frantic as to why he wasn't writing. I decided to go to Bridgwater where there was a psychic that I had heard about and was hoping she could tell me something. As I sat down in front of her, she said, "Give me something of yours." The only thing I had was a hairclip and I gave it to her. As she held it in her hands she said, "You are in love with an American Soldier." I sat there and didn't say a word. I was not going to give her any help. She said, "You have not heard from him in a while. Do not worry as he is somewhere where he is not able to write to you. He is also in love with you. Within the week you will hear from him." I paid her and quietly walked out, still not saying a word. I had gone in thinking that she was probably just rubbish, but I came out hopeful. I think back now about going to see a psychic and I still think 'what rubbish'.

Sure enough, his letters began to trickle in and by the middle of October, I received a letter from Bob dated September 29th telling me that he missed me terribly and that he loved me. Those were magical words to my ears. Then, in his November 28th 1944 letter, which I received just before Christmas, I read the words I had longed and hoped to hear. I thought to myself - so Sgt Burns, you really did love me before you left. Bob wanted to get married. Now, he just had to write to my dad to ask for permission. That was going to be a tricky one since my dad wasn't overly enthralled by Americans, but even with the uncertainty of what my dad was going to say, I was still overjoyed. Out of all the trials and tribulations of war, a romance between two people truly bloomed.

Chapter 13

The War Draws to a Close
VE-Day

The summer and autumn of 1944 brought great changes for my brothers, sister and me and my relationship with Sergeant Burns. Through the v-mail letters I had received from Bob since his departure in late June and after his proposal of marriage, we had agreed to be married as soon as possible. It was at about this time that I came up with what I thought was a wonderful idea. If Bob couldn't come to me, perhaps I could go to him in France.

I put together a plan that if I could get a job with the Red Cross as a volunteer, perhaps I could find my way into a unit that was going to France to help the wounded soldiers. There was, however, a major flaw in my plan. When I spoke to an officer at the American Red Cross office in Taunton I was told, in a somewhat brusque manner, that since I wasn't a nurse or hadn't worked for the Red Cross that would be impossible. I had made the silly mistake of telling the officer, that in addition to helping out, my fiancée was somewhere in France or Belgium and perhaps I could see him. The officer stared at me with a look of disbelief and said, "Young lady, we are sending skilled personnel to Europe, not tourists or girls who want to see their boyfriends." Obviously my plan failed.

When I next wrote to Bob and told him of my idea, the reply I received quite clearly questioned my sanity. Love was one thing, he said, but since he couldn't tell me where he was, he did not think much of the idea of his future wife wandering around the towns and countryside of France looking for him. What I thought was a great idea was in reality quite silly now that I think about it.

I missed Bob so much. I spent hours thinking about him and his fellow soldiers of the 949th who had been stationed at Hatch Park. As the weeks dragged on, I sat down one day, wanting to send him something special as a keepsake, to show him how they were all missed in the village. I wrote the *following poem, which I sent to him in September, telling him in the only way I knew how what he and they had meant to us.*

A Tribute to the 949th
By Eileen Barnett – 1944

They came, those Yanks from across the sea;
They came to fight, to set men free.

From the north, the south, the east and west,
Came the 949th, the very best.

They docked in England, up Liverpool way;
They stayed up there a night and a day;
Then the 949th with all its load,
Boarded the train and were on the road.

After the night that was cold and dark,
They found their first camp in Dillington Park.

We had no idea that there could be
The 949th in the West Country.

After a while this little batch,
Found its way to the Village of Hatch;

There in the park which stood all alone,
The 949th found another home.

We didn't have much in the Village then,
But we did all we could for this company of men.

We started a club for the 949th,
We had lots of fun up there many a night.

They taught us to dance the American way,
It made our feet ache for many a day.

They put up with things they couldn't alter,
Like English beer to them was vinegar and water.

> Then came the day they went away,
> Across the sea to France,
> And although they have gone, this group of men stays forever in our hearts;
> All I can say to the 949th,
> Wherever you roam, or stray,
> God speed! Good luck! To all you men,
> Till we might meet again in the USA

Bob wrote in response to the poem and how his unit received it touched my heart and it is one of the letters I keep in my memories of my husband.

An excerpt from my father's letter dated October 2, 1944 to my mother about the poem:

"The poem you wrote is all the talk here. Everybody has a copy of it and many of the guys have sent copies home to their families. One copy is on our bulletin board and everybody says it is the greatest tribute we have ever been paid. All the boys send their thanks and praise to you. You should be proud honey, as I am very proud of you. By the way I sent a copy to my mother, she wrote back and said how touching it was of you to do."

I know he thought he would be able to get a furlough (leave) *to come back to England before the war was over, as he felt his duties would soon wind down. That was, however, not to be the case. The letters from Bob had varied from his unrest to be done with the war and his happiness that we were to be married. He wrote often as the late summer brought great advances in the war for Britain and her Allies. He was very positive that the war would be over by Christmas and that he would then return to England and we could be married and get on with our new life together. The letter of late October, when he proposed, was I felt the greatest thing I could have ever hoped for, and in my mind I thought we would spend the Christmas of 1944 together.*

Unfortunately for my mother and everyone in Europe (for that matter around the world) the war would not end in 1944. There were many hurdles my mother and her American still had to face in the coming winter. Since D-Day the war had indeed progressed well for the Allies, up to a point. As the advancing armies neared Germany, however, the resistance of the

Germans began to stiffen alarmingly. What lay in store for soldiers and civilians alike in the final weeks of 1944 was, according to historians, to lengthen the war by months. The Allies began to experience supply shortages for troops at the front. Britain had virtually exhausted its manpower resources after six long years of fighting and military leaders made some decisions that were to cost lives and time.

Military problems had started to arise as a result of the direction the war was taking, but it was the civilians who bore much of the daily trials. They were hungry, many were displaced, and the Germans had begun a 'Baby Blitz', with V-2 rockets, on London shortly after the allied invasion, so once again the civilians of London were dying. People in many countries were still suffering from the terror of the war; the lucky ones were just worn out. The war had been going on since September 1939 and the people in Britain had grown weary of bombings, rationing, and their men still being killed at the front. At home the ongoing struggle of the war was becoming unpopular. "Let's End the War" was being heard with growing frequency.

The war at the front threatened to become a stalemate, and with the onset of winter, the successes of the summer became a memory. After the disappointing failure of Field Marshal Montgomery's Arnhem offensive in September, the euphoria from D-day waned. My father and millions of other GIs and Allied soldiers began to dig in for what looked to be a war against a more determined foe. The Germans were now defending their homeland and the final winter of WWII would, indeed, prove to be a test for soldiers and civilians alike.

At the end of November 1944, the Gaults returned to their home in Canada. With their departure, the big house seemed very lonely. There were only the four of my family, a wonderful lady named Dolly Morgan and her son Michael left at Hatch Court. Dolly's husband was serving in the Royal Marines and was stationed in Iceland at the time. It was so sad to say goodbye to the Gaults. We missed both of them very much. I then came to the stark realization there were only the six of us in the house and we would face the coming winter alone.

For reasons I didn't know, the water at the house had been cut off, because the pump in the grounds had broken down and had not been repaired. The four of us were forced to carry a huge tub down the drive to the groom's house, fill it with water, and then carry it back to the house to wash, drink, and cook with. This went on from the time the Gaults left,, and we continued this practice through deep snow and freezing cold. I continually asked Greely, who was in charge of the grounds, when he would fix the pump. His answer was, "When I get to it." It seemed he did not care much if the evacuees had water or not. After repeated attempts to get him to do something, I finally called an Estate Agent in Taunton, who knew the Brigadier, and told him if it was not fixed immediately I would send a wire to the Brigadier in Canada. Amazingly the pump was fixed within two days.

As Christmas of 1944 approached, England was experiencing its coldest winter in over 50 years. I can still remember the cold. It wasn't the type of cold you felt during a normal winter. The wind blew constantly from the north. The gales from the sea were sweeping across Somerset and created a numbing chill on everything and everyone. The cold cut through you and you stayed chilled to the bone every day. Even the simple task of walking to the farm from the main house became an exercise in endurance. My gloves were worn thin and I often wished I had taken Bob up on his offer the previous winter, when he wanted to give me his GI sheepskin lined gloves that most Americans had with them in 1943. It was a depressing time for us being alone and not having any gifts for the little boys. Finally Marie and I went into Taunton and stood in line for hours for little things like toothbrushes, soap, combs and sweets. One day I went into a local war supply station and begged the man for anything for my brothers, sister, and Dolly's little boy. He ended up raiding a 'Bundle for Britain' package and gave me some chocolate, a pair of mittens, and a book. (Bundles for Britain began early in the war and became a lifeline of daily necessities sent to the people of Britain by citizens of the United States).

We had no Christmas tree that year, but I received a letter from Mrs Gault telling me she had given Mr Davis at the farm, orders to give us two chickens for Christmas dinner. After I read the letter I immediately went up to the farm house and asked Mr Davis for the chickens Mrs Gault had ordered for us. He said he didn't know anything about two chickens and would not give them to me. I told him he was a terrible man and with that I got on my bike and left. By this time I was desperate to find food for a Christmas meal.

I then decided to go to the butcher in West Hatch to try and find something to eat. I rode on my bike in the freezing rain to the butcher's. When I arrived the butcher's son told me his mother and father were in Taunton, but if I wanted to come inside the house with him he would see if he could find something. I told him exactly what he could do with his suggestion. As I was standing outside in the rain, deciding what to do, the young man came back out and apologized as he handed me a wrapped package. I took it, got on my bike and rode back to the house. The package turned out to be a little bit of fat bacon...some Christmas dinner!

I sat down with my sister and explained to her there would be not much of a Christmas this year. With that she began to cry and so did I. Early the next day, on Christmas Eve, Marie, who had a much kinder manner than me, went to see Mr Greely to ask for some vegetables, which he gave her. With what little we had Marie and I made custard and jello (with what and from what I cannot recall). I then set off to Taunton and, with the few shillings I had left, bought a cake from a baker. When I returned to Hatch Beauchamp, I invited a few of the village evacuees to the House to share Christmas with the four of us, as Dolly and her son Michael had gone to the Greely's for Christmas dinner. Marie and I tried to make it as festive as possible for the little ones. After our 'dinner' we all had cake and sang Christmas songs, then we walked the children back to their houses singing all the way. As we returned to the House in the darkness the boys were singing, and somehow, after all the difficulties that had taken place over the previous two days, Marie and I felt grateful for what we had and for the fact we were together and safe.

It was not a Currier & Ives, or Harrods, Christmas; it was more like 'A Christmas Carol', but it was indeed a Christmas I have never forgotten. When Mrs Gault discovered what had happened she was livid, and asked if we had received the Christmas packages she had sent for us from Canada? I told her no, and she said they must have been lost in transit or stolen. She was very upset that things had turned out the way they did.

When I wrote telling Bob how things had turned out for us, he was naturally somewhat angry. He said we should have gone to his old camp, told whoever was in charge that I was a fiancée of an American who had been at Hatch Park before D-Day, and asked for some food. He doubted they would have *refused us, and that I should not have let my pride get in the way of feeding my brothers and sister. I sheepishly wrote back and told him pride had nothing to do with it, I simply had not thought about going and asking for help. Looking back, I realize I sometimes was not as clever as I thought.*

I asked my father about his time in Belgium and France, during the winter and Christmas of 1944. He did not say much about his experiences, but, he did describe a few events which added to his frustrations at not being able to obtain a furlough (leave) and return to England to marry my mother. There was one story which he related that, while in retrospect was humorous, it reflected in a small way the absurdity of war for the regular GI.

When the war reached a stalemate, his unit was detached from the division and sent back from Belgium to France. They trained in the French countryside on the outskirts of Paris and began manoeuvres, for what they were told, would be an offensive in early January. As the weather started to worsen, the attitude of the men changed with the weather. In the field, the rain, cold and mud made things miserable and waiting for their next assignment added to the men's unrest. While he found little humour in his recollection of that final winter, he did recall one event that could only happen during war that later he thought of as a lighter moment.

After a long day of training he had brought his men to a farmhouse to be briefed by his commanding officer, when he realized three soldiers were missing from his group. After asking if anyone had seen them he went back across the field to look for them. They were nowhere to be found; he realized his CO would not be happy to be told he had 'lost' three U.S. soldiers. As he made his way back to the farm house he passed a half burned barn where he could hear singing and low voices laughing. He crept up to the barn and looked inside expecting to see Germans; instead there were his three missing soldiers, quite drunk. After asking them what the hell was going on, the three happily told him they had discovered the farmers wine buried in the field and proceeded to drink themselves into an early holiday mood. My father, unable to share in their jollity as he was going to have to explain their condition to the Captain at the farmhouse, simply told the Captain the men had become ill drinking some fouled water.

My mother recalled some of the correspondence between her and my father during the last winter of the war.

I received a letter from Bob on November 1st in which he apologised for having missed my birthday and hoped next year (1945) we would be together, in America, to celebrate my next one. Unfortunately, that would not turn out to be the case.

In October 1945 Bob was still in the Army on occupational duties and waiting for his discharge. I was to spend that birthday in London, feeling rather lonely, married, and waiting for the final paperwork which would allow me to enter the United States, as part of what became known as the 'English War Brides come to America'. His next letter told me he had written to his mother in the U.S. telling her he had proposed to me. His mother, who was from Wigan in the north of England, replied saying she was pleased, but hoped we did not 'have to get married'. Bob made the mistake of telling me, because he found it amusing, but I was less than amused and found the comment difficult to forget, even after I arrived in the U.S.

In early April 1945, the time had finally arrived for the four of us to go home to London. This time it would be for good. We were so excited as we packed up our few possessions for the train ride to Paddington Station. I had asked a local baker to make my wedding cake. It was quite a chore as many ingredients were not readily available, but finally I had my traditional English wedding cake. It was beautiful, decorated with white icing, and silver horseshoes on the top for 'good luck'. I carefully packed it in a box. So with our belongings and wedding cake in tow, off to the train station we went.

The Gaults were still in Canada, so there were no official goodbyes. I had no regrets about leaving. The four of us had done our share for the war effort by staying at Hatch for six years. I had a new life to look forward to and that was the only thing on my mind. When we boarded the train it was packed with servicemen. I stood the whole way, with my cake between my feet, and swearing every time a serviceman came too close to my cake. I kept shouting, "Stand away from me, stand away." I was not going to let anyone step on my cake.

When we arrived at Paddington, my Dad and Lucy were there to pick us up. Dad had just married Lucy a few months earlier. When Dad had met Lucy the previous year, I was naturally angry. I told him in no uncertain terms, that I was never going to have anything to do with her. I just couldn't bear the thought of anyone trying to take the place of my mother. After I met Lucy, however, I felt very ashamed of the way I had behaved. She was such a lovely lady. It had been so selfish of me to have acted in such a horrible manner. I was thinking of no-one but myself. My father, after all, would be left taking care of Marie and the boys when I left for America. Now, I was pleased and relieved to know that they would be well taken care of and my dad would no longer be alone.

Dad and Lucy had moved to Plashet Grove. Once home, I went back to Plaistow where I grew up and just walked around. I didn't recognize any of it. The devastation of the bombing had taken its toll on the whole neighbourhood.

I went to the Labour Exchange and got a great job at the Food Office. Marie had just started working in Barton's Bakery, but I got her a job in another part of the Food Office. It was so close to home, we walked home every day for lunch. It was an excuse to listen to the American Forces network and all the tunes that Bob and I had danced to. I just daydreamed about the time we would finally be together.

The letters I received from Bob during the next few months in April, May, and June varied from his happiness over our upcoming marriage, to his mistaken belief the war would end at any moment, plus his hope he would be furloughed (given leave) to England or receive his discharge from the Army.

Those last two months of the war were both exciting and, for Bob, apparently very frustrating. In April, Bob's letters were full of uncertainty. We had endless paperwork to complete before our wedding, and he seemed to be sending more and more forms that I needed to sign, almost every time he wrote. In early April, his duties seemed harder, as the fighting in his area was winding down, than during the previous winter when the "Battle of the Bulge" was at its height. A few men from his company had returned to England and two had been sent back to the States for medical reasons. As I look at the letters from 65 years ago, I think he was tired, anxious, and ready to move on with his life, just as were millions of other soldiers and civilians, but as young people we always thought our problems were the greatest.

I received a letter almost every day from him, he always expressed his love and how happy we would be once the war was over. The letter I received from him on April 15th 1945, however, showed a side of my future husband I had not known. The sadness and genuine grief he expressed over the death of

President Roosevelt was very touching. I had only seen him as the tough soldier that the Americans portrayed, not a man with deep emotions. His comments about the men's sadness at the news, the church services that were held in Roosevelt's honour, and how many of the men felt they had lost a friend or family member made me realize that President Roosevelt was much more than just a leader to the American people. I had seldom known Bob to be so emotional. His letter of April 23rd explained to me, for what seemed to be the hundredth time that I was to make sure to take care of the paperwork, go to the Armed Service Centre and get my information for future transport to America, etc. I felt sometimes more like a private in his company than his future wife. He would discover during the next few months that even though I loved him, the English were not always fond of taking 'orders' from Americans.

In May, when the war finally drew to a close, Bob still wrote regularly. His unit moved to Cherbourg on May 5th and he, as did all soldiers and civilians alike, celebrated the war's end on May 8th. At that time we had finally completed the endless paperwork and he was simply awaiting furlough approval to return to London for a seven day leave. His letter that arrived a few days after VE Day clearly indicated the men had celebrated with gusto over the previous few days. In addition to being thankful for the VE Day announcement, I awaited a letter telling me when he would arrive at Southampton and be taking the train to London so we could finally be together. Suddenly, his letters in mid-May began to indicate his leave would not be forthcoming for some time. He had left in June 1944 and I had not seen him for eleven months. The letter I received from him on May 25th was to destroy all of our plans; suddenly things were 'on hold', as he said. That letter and the ones that followed in June, were heart wrenching.

My mother showed me the letters she had received from my father during those two months (she had actually kept every single one of my father's letters from 1944 – 1946). As I read them, it was difficult to comprehend how she must have felt when she heard from my father that the life they planned may never take place.

By the end of the war in Europe, those troops who served on the frontline in combat were the first, in many cases, to be discharged to return to the United States or obtain furloughs. Although my father had, by May of 1945, spent a total of 36 months in the Army, 3 months of which were in combat, unknown to him he did not have enough points to be discharged. Furloughs (leave) had been granted to a few members of his unit, due to hardship or combat wounds, but as he had received a promotion to First Sergeant in April, this kept him on active duty rather than allowing him to obtain a furlough to be married. One of his letters stated he would rather come back as a Private than not come to England to see my mother. The U.S. Army then, as now, had its own way of operating; an early release was not to be. Rather than being granted a furlough or discharge, as he expected, he had to write saying all furloughs had been cancelled. He was transferred to Camp Lucky Strike, then to Marseilles, France and was assigned to a company that was preparing to go to the Pacific. A letter of June 25th showed an unfortunate, thoughtless side of my father in his explanation of his situation to his bride-to-be.

On June 25th 1945, I received Bob's letter in which, in very blunt terms, he said he was sure he was being transferred to the Pacific. His commanding officer had already been shipped out and had told him he would leave at the end of June for training in the States, before being sent to a staging area for the invasion of Japan. I was devastated, not at his being sent to the Pacific, but by the seemingly cold-hearted way in which he wrote to me about how he saw our future. He said it looked as though our marriage would have to be put on hold and he would very probably be gone for as long as two years. But he said he would always remember me and perhaps someday we could get in contact and see each other again! He went on to say how he would always think fondly of his time in England, the fun we had at dances and to give his regards to my father, my brothers, sister, and the Brigadier and Mrs Gault. At first I was heart-broken, then after crying for what seemed like an eternity, I made the decision, this American was not leaving me behind without a fight. If he thought the war in Europe had been bad, he was in for a shock. It would be nothing compared to the fight that he was about to have with me.

The next few days were personally as painful as any I had experienced throughout the war; I read his letter over and over trying to make sense of it. I finally got control of my emotions and sat down to write my response, one he would never forget. If he was going to throw away our romance and our life together, he was not going to forget the village girl he had proposed marriage to, for a long time. At the end of June I sent him a letter that, he said for many years afterwards, almost burnt his hands. In no uncertain terms, I informed him he was not going to leave and have fond memories of me. I had gone through the last 11 months waiting for his return, I had filled out more forms than I thought existed to marry him and furthermore, I was willing to wait for as long as it took to be married. If he had to swim back across the Pacific, we were going to be married, or he would spend the rest of his life looking over his shoulder for me to come after him. This was no fleeting wartime romance like other English girls spoke of. I was in love, he had proposed marriage to me and I intended he should see it through.

As I wrote what, I felt in my heart, might indeed be the last letter to Bob, I believed I had nothing to lose. I told him he was arrogant, self-centred, selfish, and had lied to me. I also pointed out my father would soon be coming to France to visit him (that, of course, was a bluff, but in the end it served its purpose). Finally, I told him the Brigadier was friends with his commanding officer (which was true), and I was going to ask him to speak to Bob's Colonel (which was, of course, another bluff) about the behaviour of one of his men, who would send such a cold hearted letter to end a relationship.

Surprisingly, I immediately received a letter back from Bob. In typical American doubletalk, he explained I had completely misunderstood what he had said. His entire letter was based on the fact of him having to go to the Pacific. We would be married and he wanted me to remember all the wonderful times we had had and to keep the memories UNTIL he returned. He did not mean our relationship was over, he just couldn't put into words in a way for me to understand that we might have to wait a while longer. Then he begged me not to have my father come to France and he would appreciate me not telling the Brigadier. I knew then, and have always felt, Bob had a case of cold feet. However, the following letters I received said that he was moving Heaven and Earth to get a furlough, or waiting for his discharge, so he could come to

England. He asked me if I would meet him at Paddington Station the minute he arrived. I assured him my father and I would both be waiting for him.

Fortunately Bob did not have to go to the Pacific; the dropping of the atomic bomb finally put an end to the terrible war. Bob told me later that after reading my letter he might have felt safer in the jungle on a far off island than facing me. His feet apparently thawed and we once again moved ahead with our plans to be married.

As June turned into July, the letters I received from Bob were primarily centred on his trying to get a furlough and our plans for our marriage. Although he did not know it, his furlough would not come through until September. Time weighed heavily, as his duties as First Sergeant, while seemingly a good thing, turned out to be very challenging for him. His men were bored and slow to perform their duties, as they waited for official confirmation as to their movement to the Pacific. It was during the summer months that Bob's relationships with his friends, with whom he had served for the past few years, became strained due to their lack of motivation. One of Bob's closest friends, Corporal Lewis, refused to take an order and was put on KP. It left Bob no choice, but to put him on report. This coupled with other performance issues by other soldiers led to two being reduced in rank; they never forgave Bob for doing what he viewed was his duty. It was a sad ending to some close relationships that had been formed during the war years.

I felt sorry for him, for while looking forward to our reunion, he was sad that things turned out the way they did with men he considered friends. I knew these men from their time at Hatch and they were inseparable. Peace brought out a feeling amongst the men, of the war is over in Europe, let's move on to the Pacific or let's go home. The men were tired, and, as the final months of the war approached, some friendships sadly ended in harsh words. These instances bothered Bob for years afterwards.

At a reunion of my father's unit in Washington, D.C. in the early 1990s, he still felt the bitterness amongst some of his fellow soldiers from the last few months of their time in France, 55 years before. He said that sadly when he and my mother attended, what was to be the 949th's final official gathering, one of his men, who had obviously had one too many refreshments, sat at my father's table and angrily asked him why he had prevented him from being promoted at the end of the war. My father explained it was the Company Commander, and not him, who had stopped the promotion due to him not performing his duties in France after VE-Day. The man was not convinced and told my dad he knew it was him, and not the CO. As he got up to leave the table he said, "Too bad it wasn't you who got it in Belgium." A sad ending to a relationship and something that hurt my dad until the day he died. Not every story in wartime friendships had happy endings. On reading the letters my mother kept from my father, one of them mentioned the incident the man referred to from 55 years ago. The reality was my father went to his Commanding Officer and prevented court-martial charges from being filed against his comrade. The man, who died in 1998, I am sure never knew or believed the truth.

August turned into September, as the time for our long awaited reunion and marriage was approaching. In the end it took 15 months, from him leaving that late summer's evening in June 1944, until I saw him once again in September 1945 to be married. With his return we had a few more hurdles to overcome and a secret I hid from Bob until the day of our wedding.

The war was finally drawing to a close in the spring of 1945. Germany was about to surrender and we were all waiting for that long awaited word. It was the evening of May 7, 1945 and all kinds of rumours were flying around. We went to bed, still not knowing officially that the war with Germany was over. On May 8th, everyone was going crazy, but it wasn't until about 7.00pm when we heard people almost screaming and as a group of ATS girls were riding around in a truck yelling, a bulletin was heard on the radio. Prime Minister Winston Churchill announced the war in Europe was over. We all ran out into the streets. We really didn't know whether to laugh or cry. Everyone in the neighbourhood was hugging each other. Lucy made a pot of tea; we drank it and went to bed.

We were up early the next day. Gladys Mallon, a good friend, and I decided we were going up to the West End. My dad forbade me to go as he said, "There will be millions of people there and you will never get home. The trains will be overcrowded." I said, "Then we will just go to a police station and stay there until morning." I was going regardless. Gladys and I caught the train to Piccadilly Circus. To say there were millions of people there would be an understatement. You could hardly move on or off the train. You could feel the excitement in the air. For once in a very long time, everyone around us was happy. People were singing and dancing on the pavements and in the streets. There were servicemen from all over the world in their respective uniforms. They were grabbing any girl that was close to them and kissing them. You could see the relief on their faces that the war had finally come to a close.

All of a sudden, everyone stopped where they were to watch as a young man in an R.A.F. uniform began to climb to the top of the Tower in Piccadilly. Naturally everyone went mad with excitement and shouted with glee.

By 2.00pm, Gladys and I were very tired and found our way into the beautiful old church of St Martin's in the Fields. We sat down on a pew and were lucky enough to find a choir singing hymns. We stayed there for a long time, just listening and resting our poor tired feet. Then we set out again amongst the crowds. I don't think we ate all day.

Later that evening we found ourselves in front of Buckingham Palace. Everyone was shouting, "We want the King!" Then to our amazement and surprise, all the Royal Family and Winston Churchill came out on to the balcony. Winston Churchill was giving his famous "V" for Victory sign to the crowd. Again, everyone went wild with excitement and cheering. You could see the tears of joy on faces throughout the crowd.

We finally caught the last train back to East Ham and walked all the way home. It was almost 2.00am in the morning. My dad was sitting in his chair waiting for me. He wasn't cross at all, just relieved that I had made it home safely.

What a thrilling day that had been. I didn't think anything could ever top that. That was until the next day. I was standing on the pavement outside my house when a man walked up to me and said, "The Royal family will be along in a minute or two." I really thought he was crazy, but sure enough, the outriders came down the street and there was the King in his naval uniform, the Queen in a beautiful blue dress and the princesses wearing grey. I couldn't believe what I was seeing. It all really seems like a dream now.

There was also a great celebration for V.E. day which took place in our neighbourhood. People had parties at the end of each street with huge bonfires. We went down to Libra Road where we knew there would be the biggest 'bash' of all. The houses were all decorated with red, white and blue and Union Jacks were flying. There was a long table down the middle of the street with all kinds of things to eat. The women who put out the food had been saving their ration coupons in order to buy something for V.E. Day. The party went on all night long, and in the midst of all of this, a lovely American GI came walking down the street. I naturally went over to him and asked him where he was going. He said, "I just want to see how the people of London celebrate such a wonderful occasion." He was truly amazed at the celebrations. He joined in with the dancing and the singing, and he really had a great time.

At midnight, the guns at Woolwich roared and all the church bells were ringing. I feel privileged and lucky that I lived to feel that moment of great joy, knowing we had overcome such fear and survived.

Robert and Eileen's Wedding 1945

Chapter 14

War Bride's Journey to a New Life

Finally after months of waiting, Bob's leave was approved and we were getting married. We were married at St. Anthony's Church in London on September 22, 1945. Tom Milner, Bob's English cousin, who was a Flying Officer in the R.A.F., was his best man. Marie was my maid of honour and my Dad gave me away. My stepmother, Lucy, and Dennis and Charles, were there as well. I was able to borrow a beautiful white satin dress and lovely veil. I carried red roses laced with white heather. Marie and my cousin, Lily, wore lavender silk dresses and carried yellow carnations and looked so pretty. Bob and Tom wore their military uniforms and looked very handsome. And of course, I had my wedding cake, still intact. I must say, although beautiful, it tasted dreadful. I guess seven months in a pillow case stored in the pantry was not meant to enhance the flavour.

Immediately after the ceremony, Bob and I caught the train to Gidea Park at Primrose Lane. We were lent a house for our short 3 day honeymoon. On the last night, we met Tom and Gladys at the Savoy in London for dinner. We simply danced the night away, and were surprised to see the King and Queen of Greece were also dancing and enjoying themselves. He was very handsome in uniform and she in a gorgeous green silk evening dress. What a treat to watch them. Bob left the next day for Weymouth to board a ship back to France.

He returned to France and remained there until December 3, 1945. He then departed on the SS William Few back to the United States. He was discharged at Indiantown Gap, Penn on December 11, 1945 and was back with his family in Steubenville for Christmas.

Even though the war was over, things remained bleak for all of us and for most of Britain. We thought that the war's end would bring food back to our tables and normality would return, but instead, more and more things were rationed. Bread, coal and food were still real luxuries. When Bob had come to England to be married, he brought a big box of K-Rations just to show Dennis and Charles. One sad afternoon when Lucy had been out all day looking for food, she returned to find she had chilblains on her face from standing in the bitter cold for so long and with just a little piece of fish in her hands to show for her effort. We thought that my dad should have it since he was working so hard at the docks, and we also decided to drag out the box of K-Rations Bob had left, and that would be our dinner. How the Americans lived off that stuff I will never know. I guess if you are hungry, you will eat just about anything.

The days seemed to drag along endlessly whilst I waited for word that all the papers had been completed, so that I could go to the U.S. as a 'War-Bride'. Then, in February 1946, I received my orders for transport to the United States. I was so excited, but also very sad that I was leaving my family and my beloved England. I was also deeply concerned because my dad had been diagnosed with TB and was to go into a sanatorium for six months the day after I was to leave for the United States.

The original plan was for Bob to meet me in New York and take me sightseeing for a few days. But then I got a letter, just before I was to leave, saying he would meet me in Steubenville, Ohio. I couldn't understand this change of plan, until it was explained to me after I arrived. Apparently his mother had said that he didn't need to meet me because the Red Cross would make sure I arrived OK. I should have realised then, that this was just the beginning of a relationship that for years had to struggle with a jealous, manipulative woman who never thought any woman was good enough for her five sons. But nonetheless, I was excited about my forthcoming journey.

On March 21 1946, I reported to Waterloo Station at 12 noon, to be transported to Tidworth Barracks on Salisbury Plain. What a nightmare that was. Once there, we were put into grim Army barracks and German P.O.W.s were there to cook for us. The food was terrible. A few of us used to go to the Salvation Army for spam sandwiches. Some of the other war brides were absolute tramps. I don't know what the American people must have thought of them. We were there for a week for medical checks. I don't think there was a real doctor anywhere to be found.

Finally the day came, on March 26th, when we were all taken by bus to Southampton where we boarded the ship S.S. Uruguay.

By the end of 1946, over 70,000 War brides had been transported from Great Britain to the United States. With these wartime marriages came the inevitable 'red tape' that accompanies any government programme and 1946 was no different from today. To sail to America was no easy task for these young brides. The following requirements were needed before approval was granted for transportation to the U.S. One has to remember that those were uncertain times and the United States was not going to let anyone who happened to have claimed to be married to an American serviceman to jump on a boat at government expense and head to the states. So, six major rules were instituted before approval was granted. Although unpopular in the view of most of the women they were in retrospect useful and necessary.

1) A visa, passport, 2 copies of a birth certificate, 2 copies of police record (apparently to make sure you were not trying to escape the hangman), and a copy of the marriage certificate.
2) Sworn statement from husband that he could support her, with details of his salary (since most of the soldiers were not independently wealthy and were soon to be discharged and seeking new jobs. The purpose of this document remains a mystery).
3) Statement from husband's Commanding Officer supporting salary details, 10 pounds in cash but no more than that.
4) Statement from husband's family, if the soldier was not yet home, that they were willing and able to support her (in the case of most brides the willingness of the soldier's family to live up to this requirement remained open to question).
5) Discharge papers if she had served in the military.
6) Evidence that she would get a train ticket to final destination before disembarking (the question here was a fear that these thousands of young women were going to remain in the City of New York with £10.00 and do what?)

These thousands of women were taking a gamble by leaving their home, as in many cases they would never return to Britain. At the time of their arrival in the United States there were outcries from people in the U.S. that the war Department was paying for their transportation instead of using the space to return U.S. soldiers to their wives and families.

Overlooked in these protests was the real issue, these women married American Servicemen. The soldiers wanted their wives to be with them, they had fought for their country and to free other countries from Nazi oppression. It seems somewhat ludicrous that these men, and the women they fell in love with and married, could possibly have been denied a chance to start their new lives. The government had asked much of the American GIs during the war, it seems the least they could have done was to bring their wives to the United States. After all, when the men were drafted to fight, the government thought nothing of taking them from their families for the 'duration'.

All the brides were quiet as the bus arrived at the Port of Southampton. Most of them (just girls) had stopped talking when they realised they were leaving England, for perhaps the rest of their lives. There was a brief moment of excitement when we arrived at the dock and saw the majestic Queen Mary, one of the world's most famous ocean liners, tied up at the pier. We thought perhaps this would be our transport to the U.S. Those hopes were quickly dashed as we were informed that we would be sailing on a smaller, older ocean liner the SS Uruguay. As we got off the buses, we were met with catcalls and jeers from British servicemen, who were quarantined on a nearby troopship that had arrived from the Pacific. I remember feeling a little guilty at leaving our country, but most of us were excited about beginning our new lives.

The Uruguay was a nice ship. It had been refitted to carry G.I.s, and we settled in as best we could. They started to load the ship in late afternoon and the first order of business was to assign cabins for the voyage. I was soon to find out how thankful I was that my surname started with 'B'. It meant I was assigned to 'A' deck and I was to share a cabin with five other brides. The cabins had bunk beds, and I remembered Bob telling me to grab the top bunk if possible, it would be a smoother ride. He had apparently slept in the top bunk on his transporters across the Atlantic during the war. The next ten days crossing the Atlantic, during late March, I found being on the top bunk made very little difference to my comfort. When I finally saw Bob I expressed to him his advice was of little help.

All seemed well as we set sail. The tugboats eased us from the dock, and blew their whistles giving us a wonderful, if somewhat emotional send off. However, as England started to fade from sight we all ran to the stern of the ship, and many shed tears of sadness. Some of the girls looked at each other as if to say, "What have I done?" The only time I was truly scared was as we sailed south and passed Gibraltar. The fog was so thick you could not see a foot in front of you. There were many ships in the area and the constant blowing of foghorns and ships whistles was very unnerving.

We went to our cabins and for a time just sat in silence, motionless. Later we were called to lunch in the dining room. Everything looked beautiful, white table cloths, fruit on the tables and actual menus to order from. We all ordered wonderful meals and waited for our food. When it arrived I couldn't believe how good everything looked. After six years of rationing, what lay before us on the tables seemed unreal! We were all enjoying our food when suddenly the ship began to roll and roll, and roll as we left the channel and moved to open water. Needless to say the dining room emptied rather quickly. Almost everyone became seasick. I had never been on a ship before and as I stumbled back to my cabin, I prayed for a quick death. I thought ten days of this and I will definitely go over the side. Having reached the cabin, the stewards appeared and suggested to us it was better to try and eat something. They gave us some crackers and suggested we take our blankets and go for some fresh air. It was to make us feel better and as I felt as though I would die anyway from the seasickness I went up on to the deck to at least get a last look at the ocean.

Most of the girls remained seasick for days and hardly left their cabins. I remained in bed for two days, drinking cokes and eating soda crackers. As bad as we thought the first few days were, on the third day we ran into one of the famous Atlantic storms. We were all scared to death that the ship would sink, as it pitched and rolled endlessly. One of the girls made the comment, "I have lived through the Blitz, the evacuation, the endless red tape of the U.S. Army in order to marry my husband and now we will probably all be lost at sea and never reach America". As you can imagine there were very few people in our group who had any experience of sailing.

After the storm finally ended, I ventured up on deck with my cabin mates and we all felt slightly better. One of the girls who hadn't been seasick kept going on and on about the beautiful food we were missing, and described in detail the various meals she had enjoyed, as we all turned green. After her descriptions of the dining room food, we took a secret vote and decided she was to be thrown overboard if she mentioned any more of her 'dining experiences'.

As the voyage progressed we were called for health checks carried out by American nurses. Unlike the awful, humiliating embarrassments of Tidworth health examinations, these were conducted with professionalism and respect. The women were very nice, even though some of them did not seem thrilled that English girls had married their American men. The stewards were very kind to us. They knew we were not used to travelling by sea and kept us supplied with Cokes and even brought some meals to the cabins. Time passed slowly during the voyage, and some girls cried constantly, apparently having second thoughts at their decision to leave England. Others had the time of their lives, enjoying every moment of this 'once in a lifetime' adventure. Most of us talked about our husbands and the new life that awaited us. For me, I simply wanted to see Bob, Steubenville, his home, and begin my new life as his wife.

I read books, pamphlets really, about the States that were on board to help 'educate the brides' about America. I guess they were simply preparing us for life in a new country, just as I remembered Bob telling me how, on his voyage over to Britain in 1943, the soldiers attended many lectures about the English people and their strange habits. After reading the pamphlets I found it difficult to work out who really had the strange habits, the Americans or the English! Upon arrival in New York I found we English had nothing on the Americans when it came to being different. Years later, I told Bob that when I first arrived in New York it seemed to be home to every character on earth. Of course his response was, "London during the blackout was no picnic." Touché.

After ten long days at sea, on the morning of April 6th, I was standing on deck as the mist began to lift off the still rolling Atlantic when someone called, "Look at the seagulls, we must be near land!" About an hour later, in bright morning sunshine, the Statue of Liberty came into view, first as a small statue in the distance, then as we drew closer to New York harbour it rose up from the island in the harbour for all of us to see. It was one of the most magnificent sights I had ever seen. It still fills me with a tinge of emotion, even today, when I see it on the television. Every American should be proud of this majestic statue that has welcomed millions of people from the old world to the new.

What a feeling! The MPs came on board the ship and the crew went ashore. For the brides whose husbands were there to meet them in New York, they disembarked immediately. The rest of us stayed on the ship for further instructions.

We spent a frightening night aboard the ship. The crew came back drunk and tried to break into our cabins. They were trying to sell us nylon hose for $20 each and some girls took the bait. I told them, "Thanks, but no thanks." When we came back from dinner, there were big stevedores lying in our bunks. I was livid and told these creeps to get out of our cabin and I told the one lying on my bunk, "Get the hell off my bed!" He looked and me and said, "I don't take orders from a Piccadilly Commando." I said to him, "I'll call the MPs." They left and about 15 girls crowded into our cabin. We were so scared that we huddled together and didn't say a word. I climbed up on my bunk and looked over to see a wretched sailor looking through the porthole. We were too afraid to go to sleep. Girls' shouts and screams could still be heard as drunken sailors tried to get into other girls' cabins.

The next day, the few of us who were left on board went to the dining room for lunch. All of a sudden there was a terrible fight going on in the kitchen. This huge black cook ran through the dining room carrying a big knife. We all flung ourselves underneath the tables petrified. What a nightmare.

That evening, at about five o'clock, a few of us were taken by bus to Penn Station, where we were to board the trains. We were put in a roped off area only to be stared and laughed at by the New Yorkers who were standing around looking at us. We were there for about two hours and then put on different trains. Not being used to the black porters who made up our beds, we were rather scared. There were four of us travelling together. We went to the dining car to have dinner and we ordered scrambled eggs and tea. The rest of the passengers were watching us. They stared at the way in which we held our knives and forks and drank our tea. Little did they seem to understand that we held our silverware and drank our tea 'the proper way'. I went into the restroom only to be met by two women who told me in so uncertain terms that "You people took advantage of our men when they were lonely." I just gave them a blistering look and walked out.

We continued to head east to Ohio. I lay in my sleeper fully dressed all night, still a little shaken from the experiences of the last 24 hours. At 6.00 the next morning, Bob met me at the station. I was so relieved to see him. I don't think Bob understood how challenging my journey to the U.S.A. had been. I'm sure if he had realised, he would have met me in New York.

I was determined the day I boarded the S.S. Uruguay to come to the United States regardless of what lay before me. I would always in my heart and soul remain English, having a mother-in-law who was also from England (and as I was to learn had a very high opinion of herself) made leaving my home and family somewhat more bearable.

As I began my new life in April 1946 in the United States with my husband Bob, I soon discovered that although I was happy in the U.S. I missed England and my home. My father said to me on the day I left for Southampton that if I did not want to go to America I could stay in England and he would write to Bob saying I had changed my mind. At that time I remember my shock at his words. I tearfully turned to my father and said I was nineteen, married, I loved my husband and my place was with him, wherever that might be. My father sat in his chair, leaned back, took a long draw on his pipe and said, "Then you must go to America." He was a man of few words. He had not been enamoured of the GIs, but he had received the answer he was seeking. He knew he was unlikely to see his daughter again as I set off to build my life a long way from home.

That last conversation with my father returned to me many times in the following years, as I struggled to adjust to American ways and my new surroundings. Like millions of returning soldiers, Bob returned to his old job, in Bob's case, at the steel mill where he had worked before the war and where he put in long hours. What was so different from England, was the abundance of food and goods, the large homes and everyone seemed to have cars, but the main difference in America was the lack of destruction, no rubble lining the streets, no bombed out houses and no rationing. Life in the States seemed untouched by the war, on the surface that is. Men had gone off to war and many had not come back, but the way of life of many Americans seemed undisturbed.

The letters I received from my family and friends in England said things were far from being back to normal, as rationing continued and the country started to be rebuilt. Marie wrote saying she was trying to find a permanent job, my brothers had returned to school and my father, who had tuberculosis, was getting worse. I read the letters and felt guilty for leaving, but I looked at my life knowing I might never return to England and a part of me was glad I was far removed from all the shortages and difficulties that I read about. The feeling of guilt was to remain with me for many years. In the coming years, every war bride I met had a similar feeling, that we had left a part of our hearts in England, but most of us were happy to be living in the States. Whilst I knew I was where I belonged and that was with my husband, I never put behind me the thought I had walked out on my family and their lives.

As the years went by, like many couples, we bought our first house and in 1948, after two miscarriages, I became pregnant with my elder son, Keith, who was born in mid-May. I thought life could not get any better, but then one day in June I came home from shopping and was somewhat surprised to see Bob standing in the kitchen. As Bob was working the day shift at the mill, I asked him if everything was all right. He said, "Sit down honey I have something to tell you." I knew then it was something I did not want to hear. He told me my father had passed away in March, but he had waited until the baby was born to tell me, because he did not want anything to upset me whilst I was pregnant. His words hung in the air as he looked at me and said how sorry he was and how bad his entire family felt.

For some reason I felt so alone at that moment. I began to cry as I started to replay the last conversation I had had with my father just before I left for the States. Being the oldest, I had vivid memories of him and how he took care of us and how hard he had worked. The fact that I was not there when he died, made Bob's words even harder to accept. Bob looked at me and said, "I promise Eileen, I will take you back to England someday." He told me some time later, he had received the letter about my father's death and had hidden it under the carpet in our living room. He knew he needed to wait until the time was right and for years afterwards he said it was one of the hardest things he ever had to do.

In quiet moments, I sometimes thought of returning home. As I raised my two sons, my second son, Mike, was born in 1953, and took care of my husband and experienced life's ups and downs as a wife and mother, I often thought of Bob's promise to go back. Then in 1970 he made good on his promise. In June of that year, we were to return home to England, to my home and to my family. I was thrilled to be going back.

It was such a wonderful journey. I saw my sister and brothers. We rented a car, which Bob found difficult to get used to. He said he had not remembered it being so strange to drive in England during the war, but I reminded him back then he was driving American jeeps. The army had the roads to themselves and the steering wheel was on the other side. He did not share my humour at his driving challenges.

My brothers had both become successful in their own professions. Dennis was in private business as owner of an international shipping concern. Charles was working for a major British firm and later went into service for Her Majesty's Government. Marie had worked in Canada and returned to work with special needs children in Taunton. Many parts of England, and particularly London, had changed in the years since I had left. There were, however, many things that still remained the same. In the small country villages, in the village shops, and even in London, the English people we met still had the quiet demeanour and charm that I remembered as a child. We went to many villages, and toured London, like any tourist, but without doubt the most moving and memorable part of our journey was the trip I had always thought I would never make; we returned to Hatch Beauchamp and Hatch Court.

We were returning to the village and the house where I had spent six exciting and sometimes traumatic years. It was also where Bob had been stationed, where we had met, and where he had asked me to be his wife. As Bob steered the little rental car through Taunton and drove the final six miles to Hatch, many emotions ran through my mind. What would the village look like? What would Hatch Court look like, and more importantly how would Mrs Gault receive the two of us?

I had kept in touch with the Brigadier and Mrs Gault after I went to America. They had returned to Canada to live at their home at Mt. Saint Hillarie and Bob, my boys and I had visited them there. Some time after the Brigadier died in 1958, Mrs Gault returned to England and Hatch Court. When I wrote to her saying we were coming to England and we intended to visit Hatch Court, she insisted we stay with her and I readily accepted.

As we drove into the village, Bob pulled the car into a spot next to Hatch Inn. We were both silent for a moment and then he said in a very matter of fact tone, "Well, we are here." Bob got out of the car, and looking at the Hatch Inn stated, "Hell, the place looks so small." 'Typical American' I thought to myself. At first glance everything looked the same or at least I thought it looked the same. Perhaps it was because in my mind I wanted it to be the same. Hatch had become in my memory 'My England'. I had spent the six war years growing from a girl into a young woman in this little piece of England.

As the sun was setting that late June afternoon, I got out of the car and, as I looked through the massive oak trees, that still lined the grounds, I saw the familiar majestic outline on the hill, 'Hatch Court'. I called to Bob to look at the house that still looked so beautiful. He walked over to the fence and gazed up the gentle slope that led to the Court and simply said, "Damn, that place is as big as I remember!" We laughed, got back in the car and drove up the road leading to the drive at Hatch Court.

I had arrived at the one place to which I thought I would never return. We pulled up to the main entrance and as we stepped out of the car the familiar crunch of gravel sounded under our feet. I remembered that sound from the war years when the soldiers who were stationed at Hatch marched over the gravel nearly every day and at all hours.

My mind was suddenly drawn back to the present as I heard the familiar voice of Dorothy Gault. She stood at the front door, looking pleased but a little older than I remembered (I had seen her 8 years previously when I visited her in Mt. St. Hillaire). "Eileen, welcome back, how pleased I am to see you and Bob." I was startled by her welcome; after all I had not been a guest while at Hatch but an evacuee from London, who worked as a parlour and kitchen maid.

The next two days of our visit were wonderful. Bob and I walked the grounds, went into the village, and had a drink at the Hatch Inn, where we had danced and had so many fond memories from during the war. We spent many hours, after dinner, with Mrs Gault reminiscing about the war and our time at Hatch. The past 24 years had softened some, but not all of my thoughts, about how life had been, but Mrs Gault could not have been more pleasant or a better hostess.

The house was showing its age in various rooms and I soon discovered that many things had changed. The servants, I remembered, were long gone and the house seemed very quiet and empty from how it used to be during the war, but everything changes and I too had changed a great deal. Mrs Gault was now becoming an old lady and I could see she was not well.

As the three of us were sitting in the drawing room by the large fireplace, drinking a glass of sherry and talking about the war years, I thought to myself "If I never returned again, I had at least had another chance to see the house and Mrs Gault again. And this time I had visited, not as an evacuee, but as a grown woman with my husband and Mrs Gault was serving 'me' sherry from a beautiful silver tray. My life had truly come full circle.

Mrs Gault died in 1972 and Marie was with her when she passed away. Marie lived in a cottage in a village close by. With Mrs Gault's death, went my last connection to a time in my life that in many ways shaped the person I became.

My husband and I returned again to England for vacations in the years to come. These trips culminated with my younger son, Mike's, wedding in 1987 at Hatch Beauchamp. Throughout the years, as we moved throughout the U.S., the fact that I *was English proved to be a sense of fascination and interest to many people we met.*

I think as much as anything people were fascinated, or at least intrigued, by my mother's accent. As I grew up, my friends would comment on her accent and how 'different' she sounded. In a number of cities where we lived, she joined clubs that were made up of war brides. They were known as chapters of the TBPA (Transatlantic Brides and Parents Association). As the years passed the members, who for years were exclusively 'war brides', began to include English girls who had simply married Americans. The women of my mother's generation thought, they were 'nice' young girls, but not survivors of the Blitz, and none, of course, had married one of the soldiers, sailors or airmen who came to the British Islands to save the world from Nazi tyranny.

As the years rolled by, my mother became a senior member of the women who in 1946 came to America to begin new lives. I watched the transition from a distance. I was a product of all of that resulted from the marriage of a war bride who came to America. It was part of my life and upbringing, which left others with a sense of curiosity and interest.

In the early 1990s, my parents had moved to Alabama from Oklahoma for a change of scenery. Mother had joined the Birmingham Chapter of the TBPA and once again found a group of like-minded war brides who over tea, scones and the occasional mimosa, traded stories of their lives before their journey to the U.S. and thereafter their experiences and adjustments to life in the States. With my wife, I attended one of the TBPA 'get togethers' they carefully planned and put together each year. I remember saying to my wife, Pam, that we would stop by for about 30 minutes; it would surely be a quiet party with the old soldiers and their war brides who were all mostly in their 70s, we would meet a few of my mother's friends, say a few hellos, have a drink and we be on our way.

The big night was in honour of Queen Elizabeth II and of her 45 years on the throne. Well, after countless toasts, an array of food that included sausage rolls, roast beef, roast potatoes, rolls, assorted cheese plates, trifle (the English version of dessert heaven) – well you get the picture. A number of raised glasses of sherry, port and champagne topped off a wonderful tribute to their beloved monarch. We all wished the Queen many more years on the throne and the evening came to a wonderful conclusion.

I was, indeed, proud to be of British heritage and extremely proud of my mother and her friends. I did, however, spend the next day wondering if I had raised my glass to the toast from a diminutive English woman who roared, "Up the Rebels!" and insisted on a toast to, "The memory of our late and noble sovereign King George III." My wife assured me I had not participated in either toasts that questioned the integrity of the American

Founding Fathers, nor the last American King. Dull and quiet this group was not and our little visit lasted way past 30 minutes we enjoyed the evening so much.

An endearing memory, of an event that I think my mother has kept close to her heart, was her reaction to the loss of the Queen Mother (Queen Elizabeth, the wife of King George VI). As a child, my mother remembered King George VI and Queen Elizabeth visiting areas of London which had been badly damaged during the Blitz. Mother and her friends often spoke about the fact that the King, Queen and Princesses Elizabeth and Margaret remained in London during London's darkest hours, even though Buckingham Palace, their home, was also hit by a bomb during the Blitz, and their courage helped the ordinary people of Britain to maintain a fighting spirit to overcome adversity.

It came as no surprise to me when my mother called me one day in early April 2002, and said to make sure I read the next day edition of the Birmingham (Alabama) News. Some of her friends had been contacted by the local media to comment on the death of the Queen Mother. They had recommended to the paper they contact my mother for her memories as hers seemed to be the most vivid. A local reporter contacted her and her name is mentioned below in the article dated April 10, 2002. (It is reprinted with permission of the Birmingham News). It was the nature of my mother, although a longtime resident and citizen of the United States, that in her thoughts, she still remained an English girl, some 56 years later when this article was written:

WORLD The Birmingham News + **SA**

Ex-Briton warmly remembers her **queen**

By ANNE RIJISI
News staff writer

When she was a child in 1936, Eileen Burns joined her countrymen in London's streets to celebrate the coronation of King George VI and the blue-eyed, vivacious queen destined to hold the nation's love for the next 66 years.

At 4:30 a.m. Tuesday, Mrs. Burns, a war bride married for 57 years to an American, brewed coffee in a Riverchase kitchen filled with English china; then searched cable television channels to find the funeral of King George's consort, Queen Elizabeth, the Queen

Mother. "I always get up whenever anything is going on in England. I've always been a fan of the royal family. You are born with it," she said.

Mrs. Burns' eyes lit up when a camera panned crowds lining the funeral's route to Westminster Abbey. "This is what I like to see, the people who waited up to the 12 hours to pay their respects," she noted. "If I were in London, I'd be there." "Look at the Pearly King!" she exclaimed as the camera focused on an elderly, grizzled man wearing a suit and cap encrusted with pearl buttons. "He's one of the old buskers from 'the East End, an old-time street entertainer. He was probably in the East End during the Blitz." East Enders, she explained, held a place in their hearts for the Queen Mother. During Nazi bombing in World War II, she regularly visited the devastated neighborhood. The Queen Mother, she explained as the funeral procession lined up for the slow march to the abbey, often ventured out to factories, farms and the London Underground, where many of the capital's families sought shelter from the Nazi bombs. "There was no telling where the queen would be. She'd pop up all over the place," Mrs. Burns recalled.

The procession arrived at the abbey, the service began and Mrs. Burns listened intently as Britain's top clerics eulogized the dead queen. Prince Charles caught her attention. "He looks heartbroken," she said as the red-eyed heir to the throne stared at the coffin. "Prince Charles hasn't once taken his eyes off that coffin." Mrs. Burns' own eyes grew misty at the end of the service, when two buglers played "The Last Post," the British version of "Taps." She rested her chin in her hand as a grieving Queen Elizabeth II followed her mother's coffin out of the abbey.

"I really feel sorry for her, the queen. She's lost her sister Princess Margaret and now her mother," she said. "That is a shame, to celebrate your jubilee year and your mother and sister gone."

Television coverage ended as the hearse left central London for the journey to Windsor Castle, where the Queen Mother was laid to rest beside her husband. "It was wonderful, just wonderful,"

Mrs. Burns said. "She would have enjoyed it. It had all the pomp and ceremony she deserved."

The summer of 1939 changed my life forever, as it did millions of others. How could such a young girl of 12 years ever have imagined the path her life would take; the people she would meet, the hardships she would endure, or experience the joys, triumphs and tragedies of War? I have both very fond and bitter sweet memories of my life.

There are those who have lived much harder and sadder lives than me. There are those who have lived much grander and exciting lives. This has been my journey, a journey that began in the summer of 1939.

SS Uruguay – the ship Eileen sailed on to the United States 1946

Chapter 15

Children and People of Hatch

Whenever I read books, depending on the subject matter, I have always hoped for an ending that leaves me better informed and, if possible, I would like to come away feeling better about the subject matter or hopefully a happy ending.

My reading, for most of my adult life, has consisted of books on history, historical figures and the World Wars. I have been fortunate to have grown up with my mother and father who were active participants in one of the 20th century's greatest events, the Second World War. My mother and father answered countless questions, including the one question that every person of my generation probably asked their parents, "What did you do in the war?"

I always ask every member of that generation about their life and experiences during that time. Their stories are fascinating, funny, exciting, and many times heart breaking.

1st Sgt. Robert M. Burns

My father has now been dead for six years and I still think of him every day. I go to the Dallas National Veterans Cemetery whenever I can, to visit his grave; he is in Section C, Row 3, and Grave 11. My dad was a hard man in many ways and I think he would be happy where he is now. It is a beautiful place and he is surrounded by fellow soldiers, sailors and airmen. They were his buddies. They all had something in common. In whatever war they fought, they were there when their country called. They did the right thing. We should all remember that.

Anne Jane Barnett

Both of my mother's parents died at a young age. My grandmother, Anne Jane Barnett died February 22, 1941 aged 41, from wounds received in a bombing raid near the Woolwich Arsenal where she worked. Due to the fact there was no proper medicine available for her wounds, she developed toxaemia which resulted in her death. No one in the family ever bothered to find out where she (or my grandfather) were buried. In researching her death, I discovered my grandmother is buried in the City of London Cemetery, Section 61. Why none of my mother's family ever visited their parents' graves, I find difficult to understand. I was told it was because they were all so young when their parents died and that they hardly remembered their mother and only slightly remembered their father. It is easy for me to judge their actions, but following the war, England was in turmoil, and today's technology did not exist to help in the search for people or records. I doubt if many of us would want to go through life not knowing what happened to the people who brought us into this world or cared for us, but in the immediate aftermath of war, the main concern for my mother and her family was, having survived the war, how to rebuild their lives and survive in an almost destroyed country, where many records were lost and never found. As my mother has grown older, she very much regrets that her mother's burial place wasn't found when she was a young woman.

Charles Dennis Barnett

My grandfather, Charles Dennis Barnett, died on April 6, 1948 of heart complications and tuberculosis aged 51 years. He was laid to rest in Section 147, grave D-561 in the cemetery at Manor Park in Forest Gate. My mother lived in the United States and with the birth of my brother Keith imminent, her family in England decided not to tell her until after my brother was born on May 17 1948. As the birth was difficult for her, no one wanted to upset her by telling her the sad news. She was not informed until late June of that year. In 2011, with the help of a friend, Barry Brooks, we were able, after much searching, to find my grandfather's grave. It was apparent on a cold, wet, windy, February day as I stood in front of an overgrown, obviously unattended grave, that the casualties of wars do not all fall on battlefields, for some, as a consequence of war, their burial places are simply lost to surviving family members.

Marie Barnett

My Aunt Marie Barnett passed away in 1990, too early for someone as kind as her to die. She never married; she worked for many years with special needs children in Taunton. For the last 12 years of her life, she lived in Hatch Beauchamp, at 1 Lloyd Cottage, in the grounds of Hatch Court. She is buried in the churchyard behind Hatch Court (that was her final wish). She loved that house and village. I have never heard anyone say an unkind thing about her. People apparently thought a great deal of my Aunt. Twenty years later, my mother still feels her loss deeply as they were very close. War has a way of drawing people together; it was that way with my mother and her sister.

Charles Barnett

My Uncle Charles sadly died in 1996. Charles was born, as were the rest of his family, at 1 Libra Road in Plaistow and worked for the Imperial Tobacco Company and The Plessey Company where he met his future wife Maureen. Charles started his National Service in the regiment of the Royal Signal

Corps in 1950 and stayed on until 1955, becoming a Lance Corporal. In Germany he was assigned to listening posts to pick up wireless traffic from the Russians on the Eastern Germany border. Married in 1968, their son, Matthew, was born in 1971. Charles was a good man, loving father and husband. Many of his weekends would be spent touring historical sites in England with his son, Matthew, and wife, Maureen. He studied Britain's role in World War II. There wasn't a museum, old airfield, military site, or memorial to Britain's brave servicemen he didn't know. I didn't meet him until 1985, and we hit it off immediately. He took me to many places, Slapton Sands, Dartmouth, Upottery, Cambridge, Duxford, Merryfield, Glastonbury, and others. He loved England and finished his working life as a civil servant at the Home Office, where he was able to make use of his previous experience and love of history. Shortly after his retirement he passed away. He is buried in the beautiful village of Godstone, in Surrey. Somehow it seemed fitting, because, as I learned later, Godstone was home, for a time in the war, to elements of the Princess Patricia's regiment. Again, Charles' love of history and feelings for Brigadier Gault make Godstone most suitable for his final resting place.

Dennis Barnett

Perhaps my most heartfelt personal loss was the passing of my Uncle Dennis in 2006. Dennis, like his twin brother Charles, also did his National service but in the Royal Air Force from 1950 to 1952. Most of his duty was performed at the famous air base at North Weald. His stories about his service were very humorous. Britain was now adjusting to its post war life, but Dennis was fond of relating stories about his Command Sergeant who still treated the airmen as if German bombers and fighters were likely to return at any moment. After National Service, he began work in the service of a solicitor and later worked in an investment firm.

He met and married his wife, Janet, in 1960 and I think they were two people truly meant for each other. They were together for 46 years and I know my Aunt still misses him every day. I had known both my aunt and uncle since I was seven years old, when they came to America to visit my parents in 1961. Even though they lived in England, I developed a bond with him at an early age and over the years we became close friends. He has remained my definition of an English gentleman. I cannot ever remember seeing him without a tie and every morning he listened to the BBC news on the radio. He never changed his lifelong habit of 'tea and the BBC', as he used to say. He was a self- made businessman and owned his own business, for which he travelled to many parts of the world. I admired Dennis as I did my Uncle Charles. They were both well versed in English history. Dennis was the man with whom I talked politics and who taught me about the English parliamentary system. When I was older, we spent many nights solving the world's problems over a late night glass of Drambuie. Rarely does a day go by when I do not think of him; he was more than my uncle, he was my friend.

Eileen Burns nee Barnett

When people think of England, they think of Tower Bridge, Big Ben, Buckingham Palace, St Paul's Cathedral, and the beautiful countryside that defines England. These wonderful sites pale into insignificance when compared for what to me is England personified.

My mother; at 85 she has brought stories and books of England to life for me as a child and now as a man. I cannot ever think of anyone who exemplifies that wonderful country more than this woman. She is still a devotee of Sir Winston Churchill; she carries with her a sense of pride that can only be found in someone who has lived a life like hers. She is England to me. The accent, the pride and love of a country that has not diminished one bit since she left her home in 1946 to start her life as a war bride in America. Throughout my life, anyone who ever met her, within seconds, knew she was from England and proud of it. As I grew up, my friends referred to her as 'the Queen'. I can think of no better testament to this treasure that is my mother.

I cannot imagine my life without her; my wife put it best early in our marriage when she described my mother to a friend. She said, "Mike has put me on a pedestal in our marriage, right below his mother." It is out of admiration, love and respect she maintains that position in my life. She always will. She now lives with my wife and me in Texas.

People of Hatch

There are now few people from the war years left in the village of Hatch Beauchamp: **Hazel Vernon**, Mrs Gault's niece, who is a lovely woman, the chauffeur's grandson, **John Durnham,** who ,when I visited Hatch took time to find a picture of my uncles, an unknown evacuee and himself as children. It was taken shortly after all the children from London arrived.

John Townson, the son of the late **Anne Nation,** who owned Hatch Court after the death of Mrs Gault in 1972. John is, what we would call in the United States, a 'gentleman farmer'. He is a kind man, who has helped me immensely to uncover many stories, and solve many mysteries my mother had referred to relating to the war years. John is a well known figure in the village. Anne Nation, John's mother, and her husband, **Commander Barry Nation,** (in his own right a decorated Royal Naval Reserve pilot during the war) were gracious enough as to allow my wife and I to hold our wedding reception in Hatch Court in 1985. She was the niece of Mrs Gault, and both she and Commander Nation were very kind to our family when we came there that year. Unfortunately, they have both passed away and are now buried in the cemetery behind Hatch Court.

Clare Jordan Gore-Langton, granddaughter of Commander Aleric Gore-Langton, owner of Hatch Park.

Hatch Beauchamp School is still where it stood in September of 1939 (and long before that). In early 2011 I visited the school seeking some records from those early days of the war. With the generous help of headmistress, Deborah Barrett, I obtained a detailed account of the school and its children from September 1939 through to December 1942. It was fascinating to read how the school coped with the influx of evacuees from London, as well as children from surrounding areas, who for various reasons found themselves attending a new school in a nearby village. It was amazing to follow how the school handled, with typical British efficiency, the new influx of children, whilst continuing to provide an education in the midst of war. Some children were taught lessons at the 'reading room' across the road from the school. Later, this small building was for many years to be the home of my Aunt Marie and be known as Lloyd Cottage. The records revealed the arrival of the evacuees from West Ham, Ilford, and other towns, and spoke of moving the overflow of students to the Village Hall, where my mother received most of her education. They tell of a chicken pox outbreak among some of the school children, one of whom was my Uncle's boyhood friend, Sidney Budge, who contracted the disease. A doctor was summoned. My mother remembered the event for the 'evacs as usual got the blame', but this time they apparently were to blame. Sadly, there is the story of the terrible fire at Hatch Park, where a nanny of the home's owners, Commander and Lady Gore Langton, died in the fire whilst trying to save the children who were staying at the house. The death of that lady, Miss Tennant, cast a pall over the village and the school children. The records are a priceless, day to day record of the lives of children, teachers, villagers and the small school which played a significant role in the life of my mother.

The Old Hatch Inn has had several makeovers since WWII. However, it still sits on the corner of, what has remained to this day, a quiet country lane. It is a treasure trove of memories of dances, love stories and rounds of pints that were drunk by young American, British, and Canadian soldiers, who have long since joined the ranks of history and events that changed many lives over 70 years ago.

There were people, such as the **Crossley Sisters**, who lived in a picturesque farmhouse on the other side of the village. They were known as a caring family and the sisters allowed the children to play with animals on their farm. They were friends of the Gaults and kind to my mother's family. Mary married a Scottish Colonel and moved to the North of England after the war. Elizabeth became a close friend of my Aunt Marie and remained in the village until her death in 2005.

Hatch Court is being restored to its former beauty by the gracious owners **Philip** and **Melanie Gibbs**, who now lovingly care for the property. Much of the surrounding countryside remains as it did 70 years ago in 1940. Many people who were part of the life my mother and her family experienced in that small village, are long gone; they rest in the cemetery at the church behind Hatch Court, and in military cemeteries in England, America, and Canada and throughout Europe. They are part of a past that now few of us remember and few of us can truly appreciate.

Mom and Dad visit the Hatch Inn 1985

Charles, his son Matthew, his wife Maureen, Mom, Dad
Uncle Dennis, his wife Janet, & Mike at the front

Chapter 16

70th Anniversary of the Evacuees

In 2008, my Aunt Janet informed me of the 70th Anniversary Evacuees Reunion and Remembrance Celebration to be held at St Paul's Cathedral on September 1st 2009 to honour the children of the Blitz. The journey we were all about to embark upon was to lead to a hugely important day in the life of my mother, as well as my wife, friends and relatives in England and me. The planning for the trip began in 2009, with the calls becoming more frequent as the year went by. My Aunt, who was making the arrangements, was determined it would be perfect.

As she said, "I want this to be Eileen's day." She was not to disappoint. Firstly, the tickets had to be obtained (the ceremony was by invitation only and for the first 2,000 who purchased tickets) which, as for all complex events, can be very time consuming. Getting to England was one thing. It seemed buying tickets, planning side trips, gathering up family and friends to be at St Paul's and share the day with my mother was something else. I have often wondered what it must be like to plan a military operation, after this experience I came away with an appreciation of what it must be like.

In writing this book, I have learned more about my mother, her brothers, and sister and her life as an evacuee than I could have hoped to imagine. The single event that made 10 years of research, 5 trips to England, countless interviews, cross checking of facts and recollections, worthwhile, came down to one very special day, September 1, 2009.

This story began with a twelve year old frightened little girl standing on a train platform with her six year old twin brothers, and her 9 year old sister, crying, not wanting to leave their parents and not knowing where they were going. They left London with gas masks slung over their shoulders, suitcases in hand and identity tags tied to their clothes to identify them as evacuees.

They boarded a train along with all the children of Operation Pied Piper, who departed from London, bound for unknown places and events that would shape their lives forever. For six long years, they grew up away from their parents and family homes, in a totally different environment, with people who had very different values. Adjusting to this new life must have been very difficult, particularly without the guidance of parents, but fortunately they had each other.

On a sunny, slightly windy day in September, at a ceremony in St Paul's Cathedral, honouring their courage and bravery, the children of 1939 would come together again as the survivors of a time in history they will never forget but fewer and fewer are here to remember. They were to be honoured for their sacrifice and service seventy years to the day as England paid tribute in a moving ceremony on that Tuesday morning.

The alarm went off at 5am at my Aunts home in Ilford. We roused ourselves, drank a cup of steaming coffee, got dressed in outfits befitting a trip to St. Paul's and caught the train to London. As we arrived at the station, we met up with Jack Eakins, a dear family friend, who travelled with us.

My overriding concern was whether, at 83 years old, my mother could hold up to what I knew was going to be a long day. The previous night I said to her, "Mom, if you get tired on Tuesday, just let us know and we can cut the day short and come home so you can rest." Her answer was one of pure indignation; she told me in no certain terms, *"If I have to crawl on my hands and knees through London, I will make every step of the trip."* That was so typical of my mother.

As we walked down a street that led to St Paul's and turned the corner to gaze at that spectacular church, we all drew a collective breath. There standing, sitting, and talking were 2,000 plus people milling about around the cathedral entrance. No one was allowed in before 10.00am. The first thing I noticed was the vast majority of the people were elderly; some in wheel chairs, some with walkers and canes, but all wearing tags on their clothes. On the plane over to England, I thought she would look rather silly walking the streets of London wearing her tag. I couldn't have been more wrong. Virtually every one was wearing a tag and those of us who were not, looked somewhat out of place. I have never in my life been so happy to have been so wrong.

As 11.00am arrived, we were standing outside the church that had seen so much destruction during the war, but had always maintained its magnificence. As I looked at these people who had come from all over the world to be there that day, I noticed something we do not see so often in people today. You saw it in their worn faces, the way they stood, the way they greeted each other and, most notably, the way they carried themselves, these elderly civilians and soldiers of a war more than a generation ago. It is something you can't buy. It comes from experiences both good and not so good; it comes from living a life, whether as an evacuee or as a soldier, that changes you forever. It also comes from being a member of a fraternity, a select group of people who have shared similar experiences. It is called PRIDE. It is called HISTORY.

As I stood to the side and sipped coffee, I looked into the crowd and there, talking to a fellow 'Evac', I saw my mother, waiting in line to go inside. She was bursting with pride, as all of them were. They were carrying Union Jacks, flags and banners from Australia, New Zealand, the United States and other locations from around the world. They were waiting for their moment. In that one instant I had never been prouder to have been my mother's son. I looked around and many of the people near me who were looking at the vast sea of white haired people wearing those paper tags, were also wiping away tears.

As my wife and I escorted my mother inside St Paul's, I was grateful to God she had lived to see this day. If you have never been in St Paul's Cathedral, words to adequately describe it are hard to come by. Each time I have visited St Paul's, I have always felt the presence of God within the Cathedral. Regardless of any religious conviction, it is a special house of worship. Designed by Christopher Wren, it has been witness to Royal weddings and funerals and celebrations, such as the one held at the end of the Second World War. It is also the final resting place to two of England's most famous and revered figures; the Duke of Wellington, the hero of Waterloo and Admiral Lord Horatio Nelson, the victor of the Battle of Trafalgar, which was perhaps the Royal Navy's most glorious moment. Before the battle, Nelson had a flag message run up the mast of his ship, HMS Victory. It simply read, "England expects every man to do his duty." On this day, it was people with similar values who were standing before me at the Remembrance Service.

During the Second World War, St Paul's was almost destroyed when German planes dropped bombs and small incendiary explosives on the Cathedral. It was the brave rectors, the unsung heroes of the London Fire Brigade and members of the military whose bravery saved this landmark. One of the most enduring pictures of London at the height of the Blitz is the magnificent Dome of St Paul's, peering invincible through the smoke when all around was burning.

It was into this special place, my mother and our family entered that September morning. As we were escorted to our seats, we tried to take in the breathtaking beauty around us. The Lord Mayor of London and other dignitaries filed in and the service began. Quite simply the music was outstanding, the speeches moving and the dignity of it all overwhelming. All too soon it was over and the congregation filed out through the front door of the giant Cathedral.

I had my arm around my mother as we stepped into brilliant sunshine, and, as we stood at the top of the steps which lead to St Paul's, my wife took a photograph of us that I will always hold dear. I then turned to my mother and asked, "Well mom, was it worth the trip?" She smiled with a look of pure joy and said, "Yes love, it has all been worth it." We were ready to head off for a busy day in London ahead of us, ending with a dinner at the world famous, Rules Restaurant, when something caught my eye at the bottom of the steps.

There were barricades in place holding back tourists and Londoners who were waiting to go into St Paul's. People were taking pictures of the evacuees and, as if on cue, they began to clap. Not a wild cheering like at a football match or the Super Bowl, but a dignified, respectful applause. I leaned over to my mother and said, "This is for you and all those who experienced what you, Dennis, Charles, and Marie went through. I let go of her hand and let her take in the spectacle before her. I thought to myself, "Was the trip worth it to me? Was the celebration for these wonderful people who endured so much worth this day and all the planning that had gone into it?" The answer was a simple "Yes." As an American of deep English roots, I can only say, "Well done. Well done."

Eileen and Mike at Evacuee Reunion 2009

Eileen on her way to the Evacuee Reunion 2009

St Paul's Cathedral – 70th Anniversary of Evacuees Reunion 2009

Hatch Beauchamp 2010

Chapter 17

A Son's Reflections

As I grew up I found it hard to understand how difficult Mother's life had been as a child and how she and thousands of others grew to accept what was happening to them. Certain things stick out in my mind about her life. My brother and I spent hours listening to her tales about when times were tough when she was our age. Like most young people, my brother and I listened with only one ear when our parents talked about their youth, not realizing the importance of the history to which we were listening.

However, this undoubtedly led me to take a lifelong interest in the Second World War. When the first crack of thunder was heard before an oncoming storm, it would remind my mother of the entire front of her house being blown apart during one night's air raid, or how, when he left for work every night, her father would whisper to her mother, "If I don't come back in the morning, call Reggie, the area Air Raid Warden. He will be able to get hold of a casualty list before most people, so if there is a raid tonight and something goes wrong and I don't come home, he will know."

My parents talked about the war like you and I would talk about a trip to the convenience store; very matter of fact and with little fear in their voice. Once, when we lived in Oklahoma City, my mother went to a dinner of neighbourhood housewives and this rather large, well-fed and nicely dressed woman asked her, "Where did you acquire that beautiful accent?" My mother said, *"I am English and came over to the States after the war. I married my husband, an American soldier who I met during the war."* This matronly lady, who was my mother's age, asked her, "Was it bad in England during the war, or at least, was it as bad as we read about? Did you have rationing like we did here in the states?"

My mother smiled and said, *"Yes, it was difficult,"* and with a look of disbelief she said, *"Yes, we had rationing."* The lady looked at my mother and said she understood. She said, "In Oklahoma City, my family was allowed steak only every few weeks. There were times when we had one egg at breakfast and the gas (petrol) rationing allowed us to take a family Sunday drive in the country only once a month." For my mother and the working people of England, there had been no drives in the country, no cars, gas, eggs or steaks once every few weeks. When your country is being bombed and thousands are dying every week, rationing has a different meaning and luxuries are non-existent. But to my mother's credit and with a response from someone who lived through real terror, in typical English understatement, she said, *"How terrible it must have been for you and your family during the war with the sacrifices you had to make in Oklahoma City."* As we know, not one German bomb was dropped on Oklahoma City during the war. I guess it must have been a true inconvenience for that woman to endure such hardships.

In March 2004, my father passed away after a struggle with cancer. Both he and my mother knew that the end was near when he entered the Hospice Centre in Waco that spring, but she was by his side every moment, telling him he would be home soon. I guess they both knew what was coming, but I think that she, more than my father, could not let go.

My mother wrote down her thoughts some time after his death and as I read through her journal later, I realised just how overcome with grief she was after the loss of the man she had stood beside for 60 years. I discovered that, even though he had not been an easy man to live with and they faced many challenges over the years, she had remained very much in love with him until the final Friday afternoon of his life. She wrote in her journal, to no-one in particular, that Dad had not just been a part of her life, he had been her whole life and she would be lost without him.

As I read those words, my heart hurt, not for me or my brother losing our dad, but for my mother losing the love of her life. When the final arrangements for my father needed to be made, my mother by her own admission, could not make any decisions. It was to be left to my brother, my wife and me.

The first weekend after his death, we, as many families do, sat around the dinner table and discussed my parents' life together and my mother told us many stories, not stories of great importance or of note, but things that happen to couples who form a bond so close that whatever is thrown at them they can face it together. My brother asked my mother how, with all my dad's human frailties, was she able to put up with him for sixty years? Her eyes fixed on my brother and, with the look of someone who has experienced life's good and bad times, she said softly, but with conviction, *"I loved your father with all my heart."* I wonder how many of us can truthfully say that after so many years.

We learned, in those first days after my father's death, that perhaps her background and the life she had lived had in many ways helped shape my father as they started their married life in 1946. When my dad returned from the war he and his four brothers, went back to their jobs in the steel mills of West Virginia and Ohio. It was, I believe, my mother who wanted my dad to escape the mill and their life in Steubenville. In addition to freeing themselves from a domineering mother-in-law, my mother felt my father had more to offer than spending his life working in a mill. After a few years, my father quit his job in the steel mill and took a job as a clerk in a local department store and soon he became the store manager. After my brother was born in 1948, my parents left the steel town of Steubenville and moved to Cleveland, Ohio. She had, by this time, convinced my father to leave the small town and a controlling mother, to truly be on their own. Throughout my father's business career, much of his success was due to my mother and her desire for him to be his own man, by moving away and realising that they could be independent. I can truly say she was successful in that endeavour. Not only did she make my brother and me better men, she proved to have a very positive influence on my father, her husband, the man she loved.

There were times she endured with my father when she had to show the well known English 'stiff upper lip'. She said that her vision of my father would always be that of a handsome sergeant on a village street corner in the little hamlet of Hatch Beauchamp, sitting on a motorcycle, smoking a cigarette, asking her what her name was, some sixty years before.

The first day after Dad had passed away, my mother felt her life had truly ended. She had not been alone for many years and she did not know what she was to do. She had lost her sister Marie and brother Charles, not to mention her parents and many friends from the war years. She remembered her father saying to her back in 1946, in what, as it turned out, was to be their last face-to-face conversation, "If you don't want to go to America I will send word of your decision to stay." She remembered how terribly she had wanted to go to America to be with Dad, but now, not only had he died, but so had most of her family. She was overcome with the same sadness when Dad died that she had felt when her father had died all those years before. She told us we probably didn't understand, but we did. I always knew my mother loved my father deeply.

Today her room is filled, not with pictures of any recent events, but of her wedding pictures, numerous pictures of my father in his soldier's uniform and a few pictures of her family who have passed away. As I sat beside her and clumsily tried to comfort her she said, *"I have not felt so alone since that March day in 1946 when I boarded the SS Uruguay and crossed the Atlantic to come to the States."*

The few days before the service had been a blur to her. I asked her what she wanted to do with Dad's ashes when they came. She looked at me as her eyes once again filled with tears and said, *"I don't know, you can all take care of it."* We left the table to leave our mother alone with her thoughts and walked away with our own thoughts of our father.

It was time to prepare for the final goodbye to a man, who often said his proudest achievement was the time he served in the Army. He remembered the day the war began for the United States on December 7, 1941. He was at a drugstore that day in Steubenville, Ohio, with three of his brothers, when someone from outside said the Japanese had bombed Pearl Harbor. My father recalled his first reaction was, "Where the hell is Pearl Harbor and why did the Japanese bomb it?" He was 21 years old, a steelworker in the local mill, as were most of the young men his age in that town. At that moment, like millions of other young American men and women, his life changed forever.

For early March, it was a beautiful day in Waco, Texas in the spring of 2004 as I stood at my window, looking down the street. Finally, the Black Lincoln town car turned the corner and made its way to my house. It pulled up and out stepped a smartly dressed man in a dark suit. With an air of dignity and solemnity, he opened the back door of the car and gently lifted out a small mahogany box and started up the walkway to my front door.

Even though I knew why he had come and what he was bringing, I still got a strange feeling and a lump in my throat that I had never experienced before. I waited till the doorbell rang, slowly walked to the front door and opened it with hesitation. The man looked at me and said, "Mr. Burns, it is with sadness I give you the ashes of Staff Sergeant Robert M. Burns." He handed me a flag and the mahogany box. As he turned to leave I mumbled a "Thank you." He turned and said, "Thank you for the service your father provided this country during WW II. We owe him a debt of gratitude." Then he was gone. I was left standing in the doorway with 52 years of memories of my father, that Sergeant of long ago.

His life changed on December 7th 1941and led him to England, France, Belgium and Germany in the coming years. This story, however, wasn't about him, for the deeds and actions of this greatest generation have been told countless times by esteemed historians; Ambrose, Hastings, Beevor, Keegan, Pogue, and Brokaw. This story was about a remarkable young English girl from the East End of London who, my father always said had a much more difficult and interesting life than he had had as a soldier.

The war changed millions of people, just as it did my father. On his journey, he met this young girl, married her and they spent 60 years together. Not all the triumph and tragedy in war happened to those who wore uniforms. Some wars were fought in small villages and in the streets of cities, such as London, during terrible bombings. This was the story of my mother, a very determined and unforgettable character.

Chapter 18

This England

If history has taught us anything, it is that war and the excitement and terrible suffering it brings, has been with us since the beginning of civilization and sadly remains with us to this day. The defining moment of the 20th Century was without argument the Second World War. It involved millions of people, caused unspeakable tragedies, the death of millions and changed the lives of the people who survived it. Its effects are still felt today by all of us, regardless of our ages.

There were millions of people affected by WWII, who suffered far more than my family. They were some of the lucky ones (if any one who lives through a World War can be called lucky)they survived From September 1939 until May 1945, many children, from all walks of life, were robbed of their childhood. In Europe, as in many parts of the world, childhoods ended with the start of the Second World War and it was six long years before they could return to what they hoped would be a normal life, by which time, for many, their youth was over and their family life changed beyond all recognition.

It is impossible for one book to encompass the sufferings and moments of happiness that the children of the war experienced. Many brilliant authors have magnificently described the Children's War up close and with eloquence, but each life was different and every case had its own story.

As my mother is in the twilight of a long and full life, she often talks about her family, my father, the war, places she has travelled to and experiences she has shared, or keeps locked away in the recesses of her mind. What the youth of her generation suffered, we hope won't happen to our children, but sadly in some parts of the world, children are still surrounded by war and cruel events.

There is a common thread in almost every conversation with my mother; she is English and proud of it! After a few moments of conversation, a stranger will always discover her pride in her precious island, her England. Although she has lived the vast majority of her life in the United States and is extremely proud to be an American, she is at heart an Englishwoman. Perhaps the people of her generation grew up in England at a time when national pride was ingrained in their life and their surroundings.

That is not to say people from other countries, including the United States, did not and do not have a sense of pride in their heritage. Many peoples have a deep sense of national pride and they all carry with them a deep feeling of their history. But the English stand out, as a people who over the centuries have been proud of who they were and what they stood for.

During the early part of World War II, the people of Britain stood alone against the might of the Nazi Armies and Adolf Hitler. After France surrendered in 1940, there was an even greater determination. The British would face whatever was going to happen with the support of the military forces from the Commonwealth and the brave Europeans who had escaped the Nazi regime and were determined to carry on the fight under the leadership of Winston Churchill. They would have carried on alone, but with America's entry into the war, the balance of power in Europe began to swing in favour of the Allies.

Through the Blitz and continuing military setbacks in 1940 and 1941 Britain persevered. Approximately 164,000 people lost their lives during the Blitz and the Baby Blitz of 1944; my grandmother was among those who died. What my mother and her family endured, along with millions of other families, whilst devastating in many ways, simply showed the world that the citizens of Great Britain were tough and determined not to relinquish power to the Nazis.

Many people who lived through the Blitz are as convinced today as they were in the dark years of 1939-1941 that England would have survived. As an American, of English heritage, I have a sense of admiration for the people of Britain that I will carry with me for the rest of my life.

Recently I met a woman from East Anglia, Doris Ancker, who at 84, is living testament to how people faced the threat of invasion. She lived on the coast and ultimately married an American airman from the famous Eighth Air Force and came to the United States in 1946, as did my mother. She said that every single day during the early days of the war, her parents, friends, and family expected the Germans to invade the British Isles. Yet they carried on and prepared for Operation Sea Lion, (Hitler's plan to invade England) with a sense of resolve. They went to school, her father worked, her mother took care of their home. She said, "We couldn't stop living because of Hitler." Though she has been in the United States for sixty four years, she said, "I miss England every day. I always have and will until I die." Those same sentiments are echoed by my mother and the other war brides I have met over the years. With that sense of love for country, it is clear there will always be an England.

Many people in the United States have put the war behind them; the generation of those who fought in Europe and the Pacific are dying at a rate of 1,000 per day. With their passing, the struggles of what they fought and died for, fades from the pages of history. Except on Memorial Day and Veterans' Day, people in the U.S. seem to forget those who "saved the world from tyranny."

My father was one of those people, an ordinary man from the hills of Ohio, who served his country and came back with a young English war bride; he made a smart choice. She made him a better man for the 59 years they were married. It is because of her and living in a house that always remembered 'when times were really tough,' my brother and I are better people today.

When people I know have vacationed in England, they come back and say the same thing, "English weather is unpredictable, London is crowded, the people are somewhat indifferent (some have said they are almost arrogant) and there are a lot of old buildings." I have always felt sorry for those people. They are missing what England is really about. The people have a deep love of history, pride in their small island and a strong sense of satisfaction in knowing that when the fate of the free world hung by a thread, they were the only ones who stood between the light of freedom and what Churchill described as 'the dark abyss of Nazism.'

The world has changed a great deal since 1939; much of what happened then is being pushed to the back pages of history. For those who have never ventured to England I highly recommend you make the journey. Yes, the weather is unpredictable (to say the least), the food is different and there are, indeed, many old buildings and incredible statues and on some days, traffic is halted on The Mall, so that soldiers on horseback can carry out a century old tradition, of the Changing of the Guard at the world's most famous house, Buckingham Palace.

When visitors see England up close, they find the people not indifferent or arrogant, but simply English. Stop and talk to them, get out of London and see the spectacular countryside, visit a small village that has stood still with the passage of time. Talk to one of the elderly people who you see walking the street with their grocery bag, ride a bus, take the underground. You will discover what the meaning of the famous phrase by William Shakespeare truly means:
"This blessed plot, this earth. This realm, this England"

To all of those who fought, died and have experienced the pride of calling England your native land:
"There will always be an England".

Aunt Marie in front of Picture of Brigadier Gault - 1980

Mike and Pam in front of Hatch Court

References

The Canadian Army- Official Historical Summary: Chapter II, On Guard in Britain 1941, after the fall of France. The Department of National Defense, Canada.

What is Appeasement? www.johndclare.net. Definition of Chamberlin's policy of Appeasement prior to start of Second World War.

The Story of Dillington House, A Thousand Years. By Nancy Smith with permission director of Dillington House.

National Personnel Records Center. United States Army Military Personnel Records, St Louis Missouri. Service records of Sergeant Robert M. Burns

28th Infantry Division, www.history.army.mil/ documents ETO.

With permission- personal interviews John Towson, Hatch Farm, Hatch Beauchamp. Janet Barnett, Illford, England. Maureen Barnett, Godstone, Surrey, England. Matthew Barnett, Godstone, Surrey, England (2008-2010)

Evacuee Reunion Association, The Newsletter of WW II Evacuees. Issue 153- September 2009, Issue 154-October 2009, Issue 160- May 2010,

Britain at War magazine "Operation Pied Piper Remembered" October 2009

Background information Air Chief Marshal Sir Philip Benet Joubert de la Ferte', Material from Wikipedia, August 2010.

Background Information Major General George Randolph Pearkes, VC<PC<DSO<CC<MC<CB<CD. Material taken Wikipedia, May 2009

Wikipedia- WW II, British Order of Battle, August 2010

Independent Publisher of Military History, Military Press, 1997

Ocean Liners, Reeds Nautical Books, 1992. Author Philip J. Fricker

The History of RMS Mauretania; Reference - Hawes Merchant Fleets. Bensor's North Atlantic Seaway.

www.Parliament .UK Archives, research for House of Commons member A. Hamilton Gault, Member, Taunton.

The Second World War Experience Center, 2 Feast Field, Horsforth. Leeds, West Yorkshire, England
Wikipedia - Taunton Dean Stop Line Defenses, WW II, Taunton, England. Revised October 4, 2010.

Princess Patricia's Canadian Light Infantry website. PPCLI wwwforces.gc.ca updated September 29, 2010.

BBC-WW II People's War- Memories of Evacuation 1940-1944, www.bb.co.uk/print_ww2 peoples war. This was taken from the BBC website on stories of Evacuees during WW II.

The Castle Hotel- was first opened in the late 18th Century as the Clarkes Hotel. It is a landmark in the City of Taunton and reflects the beautiful style architecture from that period. For over 50 years the Hotel has been owned and operated by the Chapman family. Background information taken from The Castle Hotel, Images of England, English History, 2009.

Notes on the Blitz- taken from WW II magazine, by Mr. Michael D. Hull, Enfield, Conn. 2009

Reference Material on the Blitz taken from Invasion 1940, by Peter Fleming, 1957.

Information on Andrew Hamilton Gault- from Jeffery Williams 1995, publication- First in the Field, Gault of the Patricia's, with permission from the publisher.

Reference sources for background information on the start of Operation Pied Piper, the bombing of the East End, the arrival of the Prisoners of War from Italy. Who arrived in Somerset after the fall of Tobruk and Bardia in North Africa, 1941. The frightening return of the Nazis V-2 "Baby Blitz in 1944-1945. Anderson Shelters in the back yards of London's citizens. And the payment received for those who took evacuees into their home at the start of the war. Detail information taken from the book Britain at War- 1939-1945, by Juliet Gardner. With permission from the publisher.

US War brides@yahoo.com Information on requirements for marriage of English girls to American soldiers and transport to the United States, 1946. With permission Michele Thomas, Voyage of SS Uruguay and photograph.

OUR STREET East End Life in the Second World War, by Gilda O'Neill, with Permission Penguin/Viking Press

Churchill College Archive Centre, Cambridge, England "Churchill's early years in Parliament. Updated from Webmaster 28, September 2010.

The Friendly Invasion, Roger A. Freeman. Page 36. Published 1992. Lavenham Press Limited, Suffolk, England.

Newspaper article in its entirety "Ex-Briton warmly remembers her Queen" published in The Birmingham News dated April 10, 2002; Reprinted with the permission of The Birmingham News – 2009.